TORK & GRUNT'S GUIDE TO GREAT PRESENTATIONS

Arrows not Bullets

Bob Harvey

Marshall Cavendish
Business

Copyright © 2008 Bob Harvey

First published in 2008 by:

Marshall Cavendish Limited
5th Floor
32–38 Saffron Hill
London EC1N 8FH
United Kingdom
T: +44 (0)20 7421 8120
F: +44 (0)20 7421 8121
sales@marshallcavendish.co.uk
www.marshallcavendish.co.uk

A CIP record for this book is available from the British Library

ISBN 978-0-462-09924-8

Cartoons by David Mostyn

Designed and typeset by Phoenix Photosetting,
Lordswood, Chatham, Kent

Printed and bound in Great Britain by
CPI Mackays, Chatham, ME5 8TD

Contents

Introduction

Tork & Grunt's Guide to Great Presentations: Arrows not Bullets is the second book in Tork and Grunt's series on modern business skills. Following their first meeting in *Tork and Grunt's Guide to Effective Negotiations*: *Mammoth Strategies*, these two cavemen have brought their tribes together to live.

This second book talks about presentations and you will see how Grunt rises to become chief of the tribe, with an expectation that he will be a great leader of his people.

Like most people, Grunt doesn't like the idea of public speaking – but with the guidance and common sense of his wife, Natter, and his colleague, Tork, he quickly becomes a competent and convincing speaker.

Grunt learns that you win with arrows, not bullets. You win by pointing the audience in the right direction, not by hitting them with onfusing 'bullet point' statements.

in this book, Naomi takes up her position as Finance Director at thyst and Jacqui heads up the launch of a new product range at ernational trade show.

The three sections of this book will teach you how to write your presentation, how to illustrate it, and finally how to deliver it.

The book incorporates some of the very latest thinking on the use of MS PowerPoint®, and explains how frequently, as in so many areas of communication and management, '*Less is more*'.

Prologue

The meeting of the tribe

The slope of the hillside made a natural amphitheatre in front of the smooth shelf of rock. The mountain rose steeply behind, so that voices carried well. Alto, the elderly chieftain, was holding court, his left hand grasping the talking stick that gave him the right to speak without interruption. Nobody else could speak unless Alto yielded the talking stick to that person. It was a formality the tribe had developed to bring order to these tribal gatherings.

On the grassy slopes before him, the crowd was sitting patiently, listening politely, awaiting the important announcement that had been talked about. He had been speaking for the best part of an hour, and the crowd were starting to become restless. So far there had been little of particular interest. At the back of the audience, ~aning back against a cluster of large boulders, Tork and Grunt were ~ing with their families, listening dutifully.

 ᴊlanced at his notes and smiled at the crowd:

  ᴀlly, *dear* friends ...'

  ᴠe *Tork* a sidelong glance:

    ~ny times has he said "Finally"? I'm bored out of my skull.
    ~etting hungry.'

The tribal meeting

Tork grinned but before he could reply, Natter gave Grunt a sharp dig in the ribs:

'For goodness sake, Grunt, show some respect for the elders. I think I know what he's going to say, so listen up now! There's been a lot of talk amongst the women about a very special announcement.'

Alto cleared his throat and took a sip from a cup of water.

'Finally, dear friends, I want you to know that the time has come for me to step down from my role as leader of the tribe. If I have one message to hand on to you it is this: "We must learn from the past and live in the future." It is time for me to hand over to younger blood than mine, and I have given much thought as to who might take on this role in the future.

'*We all remember how Grunt, from the people who lived in the valley, first met up with Tork from our people on the mountain. We remember how they became friends and together persuaded us to live as one tribe. When the time came, you elected me, as one of the most senior members, to be your leader. Now I am old and want to enjoy my time relaxing with my grandchildren. You must choose again, and I want to suggest to you that this job should pass to a man from the valley. We live as one community but we come from two cultures, and it is timely that a person from the valley should now become our leader. After much considera-tion it is my suggestion that Grunt should succeed me and be your choice as chief.*

'*There will be others who will want to contest the position, so I will say no more at this time, except to recommend that we should take that decision at our meeting which will be at the time of the next full moon.*

'*Enough, now. You are hungry and thirsty, and I thank you for your patience and attentiveness.*'

Grunt stared at Natter, who met his eyes with a proud, admiring stare:

'*There, husband. I thought Alto might say that. I was talking with his wife and sisters last week, but we dared not say anything before it was official. Congratulations, my man, you will be a good leader.*'

Grunt looked at Tork, then realized that across the hillside everyone had turned to look at him. Some were applauding politely, some cheered; others stared with expressions that did not disguise their obvious hostility. Grunt looked back to Tork and stuttered:

'*You'll have to help me out, old chap. I'm useless at making speeches. You've always been the one to talk to the crowd. I'm hopeless!*'

PART ONE

Form, content and structure

Introduction

A successful presentation needs content – the subject of this section – and it needs delivery, which is the subject of the third section of this book. The second section would have baffled most of the great orators of the past; it deals with the modern dependency on illustration, usually in the form of PowerPoint which has become the *sine qua non* of today's business communication.

In writing about content and the way it can be structured, we are going back to basics and considering what you want to say – before we start to look at dealing with the nerves and anxieties at which most Presentation Skills training courses start.

You wouldn't have lived long enough to read this book if you didn't know something about breathing, and it doesn't take a whole book to encourage you to project your voice.

Presentations and public speaking are not the problem you think they are; you just need to absorb a few basic principles and – most importantly – to put them into practice.

If you can hold a conversation, talking about something that interests you, then you can make a presentation. But first, you have to work out what it is that you want to say.

1

The risks and opportunities of speaking out

Why worry?

By the time you are three years old, you can walk and talk. Nobody teaches you. You learn by experimentation and encouragement.

As you enter formal education, your communication skills improve with language and vocabulary but self-confidence does not always grow at the same rate.

By the time you reach adolescence, your personality is evolving rapidly. Unfortunately, self-esteem often lags behind. With the onset of hormonal changes, personal communication takes on a new dimension. You become attracted to people in different ways and the nature of your interpersonal relationships alters.

Now your confidence is even more under threat. Many of those who were boisterous babies and noisy children often become shy teenagers or aggressive youths as they enter the world of adulthood. They need new kinds of communication skills; and it is largely the peer group and the social environment that will set the example.

You've been through all of this and you cringe at some of the embarrassing situations that you experienced. In particular, there was probably that first occasion when you had to stand up and speak out. Maybe you found it easy in primary school, but as you progressed through the system, it became more difficult – especially if it involved speaking to a group of strangers.

Maybe you could talk easily about sport but had difficulty talking about work. Maybe you could talk about other people's problems but could never find the courage to talk about your own situation.

So, what is it that you are afraid of?

Handling the fear

Faced with the Great Depression in 1933, Franklin D. Roosevelt made his first inaugural address incorporating the famous words: *'The only thing we have to fear is fear itself.'*

His point was that fear debilitates; fear stops you doing anything and it can be paralyzing.

In your mind's eye, think for a moment of a rabbit caught in the glare of headlights. Perhaps that is how you feel when you stand to address a group. You are frozen by fear, your throat is blocked and the words just won't come out.

What you fear is your inability to handle the situation. If you can step through that fear you can take action. But as long as your mind is captivated by fear, you are incapable of doing anything.

In 2003, I watched with great sympathy as a fellow-contestant in the International Public Speaking Championship in Atlanta, Georgia, lost his train of thought and was completely frozen by fear. He could not continue. His eyes stared blankly as he searched for the memory of the speech he had rehearsed over and over in the preceding weeks. Finally, he gave up and left the stage, biting his lip to hold back tears of disappointment and shame.

What reaction would you expect from the audience? They would have cheered a brilliant speech – what would they do now?

The reaction was immediate. They knew the pain that he was going through and they rose together to give him a standing ovation. His fellow-contestants gathered about him to put an arm around his shoulders and offer words of commiseration and encouragement. Every person in the hall could identify with that man's feelings and the situation in which he found himself. Most people had at some time experienced that churning, nauseous, paralyzing fear. Even at the highest level of the world championship, a speaker might be overwhelmed by the occasion and have to withdraw.

The reality is that there is nothing to fear except being afraid. Nervousness is a good sign: it shows a lack of arrogance and in a later section you will learn about the positive contribution of nerves to achieving a good performance.

So, what is the fear all about? What is so scary about talking to a group of people? What's the worst thing that could happen?

The five risks of speaking out

If you are not – at least to some extent – nervous when you face an audience, then you will probably not do a good job.

This applies to what is grouped in this book under the general heading of **speaking out** and is relevant to many different situations – including performing on stage to the public, making a presentation to a peer group, delivering an address to a group of strangers, or making a speech at a wedding.

Nerves get the adrenalin going, and adrenalin drives performance every bit as much for a speaker as it does for an athlete.

The root of the issue is that people generally don't like taking risks. The fear you feel comes from facing what you perceive to be a number of risks, and from what you believe might be the adverse outcome of these risks.

However, when you consider the risks carefully, you'll see that these risks actually represent some wonderful opportunities. And if you don't take the risks, you'll miss out on those opportunities.

The first risk of speaking out

The first risk you face if you speak in public is *exposure.*

In all probability, you live a private life: you decide how much people know about you. However, it follows that the more people you know, the more people there are who know you. The more people that know you, the more friends you are likely to make. And you can never have too many friends.

Consequently, it follows that you *will* have more friends – which is a good thing – if you reveal yourself to more people and that is what's scary.

Despite this rather obvious conclusion, the very thing that scares many people about public speaking is the idea of revealing themselves to a group of people, being conspicuous, and standing in the virtual spotlight.

The first risk of speaking out is that you will come out of hiding and be exposed. The implied opportunity hidden in this risk is that you will show people who you really are.

When a new business is to be launched, whether it's you as a sole trader or a new division of a global empire, it needs to advertise and promote in order to be successful.

In the world of entertainment, wannabe stars will do almost anything to attract the media, create exposure and achieve celebrity status. Maybe you recognize this need to raise your profile in the media; maybe that idea fills you with dread.

Don't worry: *HELLO*! magazine won't be after you just because you talk to your team about sales in the north-west division.

What will happen when you talk is that your team will learn more about you and get to know you better. If you risk exposure to an audience – whether it's a group of a dozen or an audience of hundreds – you can have the benefit of showing people who you are, and not just being a name on an email.

You can still be as private as you choose to be most of the time.

The second risk of speaking out

The second risk of speaking out is that you'll probably be doing something different from what you usually do.

When you were a child, you were always doing new and different things; life was full of creative exploration. You could live in a make-believe world full of limitless possibility.

Then came adulthood, and the daily routine of the grown-up world. What happened to the creativity, the ingenuity and imagination that had fired the learning and development of youth? It just faded away.

By the time they are in their twenties, most people live a routine existence, at least as far as their work is concerned. They are doing things they are told to do, following procedures and processes into which they have very little input.

In exposing yourself by making a presentation, you create the opportunity to apply the individuality and creativity that you have been obliged to neglect for a decade or two. Even if your presentation is largely numbers and percentages, you can communicate these more effectively if you move back into the world of theatre and use the vehicle of imagery and story-telling that is, as you will learn in later chapters, the basis of every effective presentation.

The second opportunity of speaking out is the chance to be creative, get out of a routine that is dominated by process and procedure, and show the individuality that corporate or institutional organizations often tend to strangle and suffocate.

Grunt worries about the risks of having to face the electorate

Grunt was sitting by the lake, poking a stick in the water, and lost in thought, when Tork walked up breezily and sat down beside him.

'Hello there, Grunt, you're looking very thoughtful. What's on your mind?'

'That's a silly question. You know what's on my mind. I'm worried about the hustings.'

'You don't want to worry about that, old chap. A week ago you didn't even know what a hustings was.'

'And now I do! It's a big meeting when all the people from both of the tribes will hear me talking about my election campaign and will probably ask me questions.'

'So ...?'

Tork tried to adopt an expression that would show his real concern for his best friend. He spoke more gently and put his hand on Grunt's shoulder:

'So what's the problem, Grunt? You've always wanted to be the leader of the tribe, you always said that Alto never really understood your people and never listened to anyone from down in the valley. This is your big chance!

'Most of our people think you're a great chap. You've always been very popular with your own people. And you've got Natter, she's a smashing woman. You know your wife will make an excellent First Lady.'

Grunt heaved a sigh and swished the stick in the water:

'It's all so risky, Tork. I don't like taking risks.'

Tork stared at Grunt with a beaming smile:

'It's exciting, Grunt. It's a great new opportunity ...'

'To make a fool of myself, you mean.'

Tork jumped up, pulling Grunt to his feet and looked him straight in the eyes.

'No, Grunt, no! This is when people really get to know you. Not when you're fooling around playing with the youngsters, or out with the men after a good day's hunting. That's the only Grunt they know at the moment. They don't know you the way I do. I know you're a great diplomat, a brave leader and a wise administrator. That's what they'll see when you take the platform at the hustings.'

Tork tries to allay Grunt's fears

Grunt glared back at Tork:

> *'But I've never done any of this! I've never had to persuade people to follow me.'*

> *'Now you're being silly, Grunt. After you and I met up all those years ago, it was you who persuaded your people to come up from the valley and make their home with us, wasn't it? What is it that you're worried about?'*

Grunt furrowed his brow and poked the dust with his stick:

> *'I was excited, back then. I was determined that we should make a success of living as one tribe and cooperating.'*

Tork quickly replied:

'And speaking was easy because you were passionate about what you were talking about. None of us has a problem standing up and talking about the best design for spears or—'

Now Grunt was starting to understand and interrupted:

'Or arguing about the best way to trap a mammoth. I suppose you're right. It's an opportunity to do something different. A bit of a change from being just one of the hunters.'

Tork slapped Grunt heartily on the back:

'Exactly! The tribes are waiting for some new ideas, fresh blood, a new perspective. This is your big opportunity to talk about all those things you and I have been saying when we get together. Everyone's bored with Alto's leadership: it's been solid and secure but so unimaginative! Grunt, old man, this is your big chance. It's not a risk. It's an opportunity!'

'But suppose I get it all wrong? What then?'

The third risk of speaking out

Of course, there is a risk attached to doing something different, and it is a risk that handicaps everything you do in adulthood. The third risk of speaking in public is the risk of what you see as possible failure.

Failure is a word you would generally use as your negative judgement of an outcome, your verdict on an experience.

Alternatively, to put this in the language of Neuro-Linguistic Programming (NLP), if you call an outcome a failure you are putting an *interpretation* on an *observation*. You see things happen in your life and you choose to label them not as 'events' but as either 'success' or 'failure'.

Somewhere along the line you seem to have forgotten that you learned to ride a bike by falling off, you learned to write after pages and pages of illegible hieroglyphics, and you learned to walk by falling on your backside.

Life is more logical when you take the emotion out of the equation and look at things objectively. This means making a distinction between what you observe, and what you feel about what you observe. So much of what happens in life is just part of the learning process, yet you choose to judge it negatively with the word 'failure.'

Replace the word *failure* with the word *feedback* and remove the judgement. Immediately, you have a different perspective on the events in your life. There are times when the only way to know how to do something well is to start by doing it less than perfectly well. That's how you learn what works and what doesn't work.

What Grunt is afraid of is not failure; it's the anticipation that the learning experience might be painful.

The choice is yours, and it's just like learning to swim. You can study the theory, you can be reassured by learning how to doggy-paddle in the shallow end of the swimming pool with one foot on the floor and your head above water, you can watch others who are splashing around enjoying themselves.

However, sooner or later you have to face your fear and jump in. That's all there is to it.

The third risk of speaking out is that you might learn something.

The fourth risk of speaking out

While the third risk is that you believe that people might see you as some sort of failure, the fourth risk is the logical alternative. For some reason, you might find this outcome even more scary than 'failure'. The fourth risk of public speaking is that people might be informed and entertained by what you say; they might see you as a success.

Nothing attracts recognition, promotion and reward more effectively than the demonstration of competence. When you take the risk of making a presentation to a group, there is the risk of success: the possibility that you might move yourself up the ladder, finding yourself next in line for promotion and advancement. Had you been content just to jog along, doing your day-to-day work as one of the crowd, then the fourth risk can be something of a worry.

What you may find is that others see in you – as a result of your presentation – strengths and abilities which they had not seen before. Maybe you hadn't even been fully aware of these talents yourself.

The objective perspective of the audience has highlighted aspects of your character that had previously been kept in the dark.

There can be downsides to demonstrating success, as any married couple knows. When one partner demonstrates competence in a particular domestic chore, it's not long before it becomes their exclusive responsibility. This is why I have always striven – with complete success – to demonstrate my inability to iron shirts to an acceptable standard.

Balancing the risks and the opportunities

➢ When you make a presentation or a speech you risk exposure. This means people might get to know you better
➢ When you're faced with doing something out of the ordinary, such as public speaking, you risk having to do something unfamiliar. This means that, for once, you have an opportunity to be imaginative and creative
➢ When you face the prospect of standing up and addressing a group, you run the risk of getting it wrong. This is, in fact, just one step along the learning curve towards making a better job of it next time
➢ If you try to learn from experiences, then in a relatively short space of time you will probably be able to deliver a presentation that is informative and entertaining. Do this, and there is a real possibility that people's opinion of you will improve and you will find that the audience holds you in higher esteem. This could mean an increase in the awareness of your business, the ability to attract support from new stakeholders, or increased responsibility as an employee – together with the associated rewards

One final risk

What is clear is that four frightening risks can also be seen as opportunities. Perhaps you see them as rather challenging, but they are opportunities, nonetheless. And each of these opportunities offers a significant, positive benefit.

However, there is one overwhelming risk that could outweigh all the benefits. There is the risk that if you DON'T face the risks and speak out, then you may never seize the opportunity to explore your full potential.

Go for it!

Tork gave Grunt a playful punch on the arm.

> 'It's your big chance, Grunt. Alto has nominated you and most people like you a lot. Just be yourself, let them see who you really are and **go for it**! You may not get it all right first time. Nobody expects that, but you'll never learn unless you do it.
>
> 'My personal opinion is that it won't be as tough as you think. People will see you in a new light and appreciate the sort of person you really are.
>
> 'It's OK to be nervous. Don't you think Alto was nervous when the two tribes first came together? Our people weren't sure whether your people might rise up and start a fight. Of course Alto was nervous and he lost his way more than once when he tried to explain his ideas. It didn't matter then, and it won't matter tomorrow at the hustings. There's just one thing you have to decide.'

Grunt had been starting to feel more confident – but now he wondered what it was that Tork was going to bring up; surely not more risks and so-called opportunities. He looked at his friend quizzically:

> 'So, what else do I have to do? Isn't it enough just to show up and speak out?'

Tork was exasperated and wondered if he could ever make an orator out of Grunt.

'Yes, of course, in simple terms that's enough and that's what I've been trying to tell you. Don't worry too much, just show up and speak out. However, the point I am making is this: when you speak out, what are you going to say? What do you want people to do when they walk away from the hustings? That's the biggest question for you right now.'

But Grunt still wasn't getting it, and he gave Tork a bewildered look.

'Is that important, then? Surely they'll do whatever they were going to do anyway? I'm not sure I understand what you're getting at, Tork. You're going to have to help me on this one.'

Tork pulled a wry face. This wasn't going to be easy.

Summary

The risks of speaking out ...

➤ The risk of exposure, which brings with it the opportunity to reveal your true personality
➤ The risk of having to do something different. This embodies the opportunity to use the imagination, individuality and creativity that you always accessed easily as a child
➤ The risk of failure, which is the opportunity to go through the learning process
➤ The risk of success, which leads to the opportunity for personal advancement

and the risk of NOT speaking out ...

➤ If you don't seize the opportunities of speaking, you will never explore your full potential

2

Why speak?

The messenger and the message

Speaking out can be a genuine opportunity for you and could deliver some significant benefits, but that's not why you do it. That's just a by-product of the exercise, although there are some people, including many politicians of all hues who never miss an opportunity for exposure to an audience, whatever the cause or the occasion.

Speaking out is about communicating a number of things. Most people think that it is only about the message that you want to put across. It's far more than that.

It's about the proposition that you are laying before your audience, it's about the organization you represent, and it's about the under-lying issues. And because you are the messenger who is bringing the message, it's also, inevitably, about *you*.

Suppose you are working for a charity whose work is with the elderly, and that you are talking about the need to recruit volunteers who will visit old people who live alone. Your audience will be evaluating their response in four areas:

1. To some extent, their initial focus will be on the **Proposer**. In this case, that's you – the person doing the talking. As you have seen, this gives you excellent opportunities for your own personal development.

2. The audience will be listening to what you have to say, and evaluating the **Issue**. In this case, it's the plight of elderly people living alone.

3. Together with their opinion of you and the issue you are talking about, they will form an opinion of the **Sponsor**. That's the organization, in this case the charity, on whose behalf they are being addressed.

4. Finally, they will evaluate the **Message**. That's what the audience is being asked to do about the issue, the specific action that the sponsor is proposing.

Based on their evaluations of all four areas, the audience will decide whether or not to respond to the presentation by taking the action that you are requesting. However, even if they don't step forward to volunteer, there will be spin-offs which may ultimately prove to be every bit as important. If your presentation is effective they may well *think* differently – even if they don't respond with action.

Another likely outcome is that the audience will evaluate the four elements in relation, each to the other.

A popular celebrity can greatly improve public awareness of a little-known issue. On the other hand a well-known person can have a reputation tarnished by agreeing to speak on behalf of a dubious sponsor.

In the scenario described, of promoting an issue on behalf of a charity, the most important beneficiary in terms of image, opportunity and heightened profile is the sponsor, the charity you are representing. At the end of the presentation the audience will have heard enough to form an opinion about the merits of the organization, or to revise any thoughts they might already have had.

Next, there is the issue that you have been talking about. You will have turned the spotlight on to a particular area and made more people aware of a situation about which the charity holds a definite position. As a result of your presentation, more people will not only know about the charity, its work and its principles; they will also have their thinking focused on what the charity sees as a key issue that needs tackling.

But all of this is still just the by-product. The main intended outcome of any presentation is to get people to think differently and/or act differently.

In this case, it is to raise the profile of the charity, to raise awareness of the issue, and to promote the strategy of calling for volunteers who will visit old people living alone.

At the nub of every presentation (and the word presentation is used in the broadest possible sense) is the need to establish a strong identity for all the elements listed above.

The **Proposer** is identified as the embodiment of the **Sponsor**, the Sponsor is identified as the power behind the **Issue**, and the two jointly become the protagonist putting over the **Message**.

If that all sounds a bit obscure and highfaluting, then think about the Best Man at a wedding. The **Sponsor** of the Best Man's speech is the Groom. The Best Man is the **Proposer**, the **Issue** is the personality of the newly-weds, and the **Message** is a favourable image of the bride and groom, symbolized by the **Action** – which is to invite the assembled company to rise to their feet and drink a toast to them.

Yes, even the Best Man's speech has a distinct objective: when he has finished speaking and the assembled company stand up, they should have a different idea – a *better* idea of the personality both of the Groom as a close friend of the speaker, and of the Bride and Groom as a couple.

Whether you are a man speaking out in support of his best friend and his new wife, or a woman arguing on behalf of a charity about which she feels passionately, or whether you are making a presentation as the Finance Director delivering the annual results, what you ultimately want is to make a difference. You want people to think differently or do things differently.

Speaking out is all about making changes, as you can see if you look back at the records in history.

Famous speeches

William Shakespeare put fine words of fiction into the mouths of historical figures. You grew up believing that Mark Antony really did talk about coming to '*praise Caesar, not to bury him*'.

It's the same for many other famous orations. You've only learned about them through hearsay, but they are nonetheless totally plausible and fit with your perception of what was happening at the time.

You can perhaps imagine Matthew, sitting in the crowd at the Sermon on the Mount, trying to remember some of the key phrases that he went on to record and hand down to future generations in his gospel:

> *You are the salt of the earth*
>
> *Don't cast pearls before swine*
>
> *Turn the other cheek*

When it comes to more recent addresses, you can read the actual words of everything said in the British parliament since the beginning of the twentieth century, and peruse fairly accurate reports of the debates from as early as 1771.

You can listen to the voices of Gandhi and Churchill on audio recordings, and watch video tapes of the way that Kennedy and Mandela delivered their thoughts.

Famous speeches are worth analysing. Some speakers have gone down in history for phrases that in time became famous. Winston Churchill talking of '*Blood, toil, tears and sweat*'; Martin Luther King's '*I have a dream ...*' and the famous words of John F. Kennedy at his inauguration as US president: '*Let us never negotiate out of fear. But let us never fear to negotiate.*'

Later in this book, you will study the text of Abraham Lincoln's Gettysburg Address and see how this short speech (only 296 words) not only includes several memorable phrases, it is also an outstanding example of structure, metaphor and messaging.

Why do speeches survive through history?

Whether you are looking at actual speeches, such as the words of these world leaders, or fictitious ones, such as the words that Shakespeare chose to put into the mouths of past heroes ... why do they survive?

Historical records of speeches have survived for the same reason as has the great tome known as the Domesday Book.

It's because they were essential steps in the process of fundamental change. These memorable words were delivered with the intention of starting a course of action that would make things happen and bring about change.

The Domesday Book was drawn up in 1086 as a record of all the land-holdings in England at the time of William the Conqueror. It was compiled to facilitate the assessing of taxation.

Happily, most speeches these days have less draconian objectives. Nonetheless, every time that someone speaks out with a presenta-tion, an address, in a debate or delivering a lecture, the core purpose must be a call to some sort of action.

You might think that there would be an endless list of the sorts of action stemming from a speech. In fact, they are all designed to insti-gate change, and these changes can be summarized into just two categories of action:

1. Speeches are asking the audience to *think* differently, or
2. Speeches are asking the audience to *act* differently.

In short: speeches are aimed at *changing the mindset of the audience.* And before you plead that speeches sometimes implore the audience NOT to do things any differently, I would add that on such an occa-sion the plea is made to persuade the audience to take a different kind of action and reverse the prevalent trend. The audience is being encouraged to do things differently from the way things appear to be going.

For this reason your presentation, whether it's the Annual Report to the shareholders or the Best Man's speech at a wedding, must end with a call – overt or implicit – for an active response from the audience.

This could be an actual physical act:

> '*It's the Superbowl*! *Go out there and score*!'

Or it could be asking the audience to adopt a particular attitude – as when Bradley, Managing Director of Amethyst Holdings, introduces Naomi at the annual management conference:

> '*I want to introduce Naomi, who joined Amethyst last year from JK Engineering as our new Finance Director. This is the first of our company conferences that she's addressed, so many of you will not have had an opportunity to meet her. I would like to take this opportunity to give you some background before she delivers the financial report.*
>
> '*Naomi comes to us with outstanding academic and professional credentials and a first class track record ...*'

No speech should ever be the bare presentation of a schedule of facts. You must tell the audience what you expect them to do with these facts. And every single time, it should be either to think differently or to act differently.

Naomi doesn't want to be boring

During her time at JK Engineering, Naomi had indeed established an excellent track record. She had proved herself an able negotiator in dealings with Amethyst, which is probably why Bradley had the idea of making the initial approach to see whether she would jump ship and join the expanding management team at Amethyst.

The first months had gone well: she had been able to put her personal stamp on her department. She was particularly keen that her first appearance at the national conference should go well. Consequently, she decided to meet up with her uncle James, who had retired from a senior position in a global company.

His job had meant that he travelled the world, often making presentations to company meetings wherever he was. Naomi was sure that he would be able to give her some useful advice and guidance on how to ensure that she came across well.

Naomi took the train up to Anchorford, the sleepy little town to which James and her aunt Sophie had retired, and breezed into the lounge of the Station Hotel.

'Uncle James, how lovely to see you again!'

'Please Naomitik, just call me James; that way I don't feel so old. Let me get you a drink. You must be weary after that train journey?'

'Oh, I'll never get used to calling you just James – but if you insist. You take me back a few years, calling me Naomitik; it was always your name for me when I came to stay with you in my school holidays.'

'Those were lovely times. But that was years ago, wasn't it? Now you're the FD of an expanding company, I hear. How's it working out? Look, about that drink. First things first.'

'I'll have a G&T please, ice and lemon. Thanks, that would be most welcome after the journey. I must say, I love it at Amethyst and it's going really well.'

Naomi settled in the comfortable lounge while James fetched her a gin and tonic from the bar. As he returned she launched straight into the reason for the visit.

'You know why I wanted to meet up again. I need to pick your brains about the presentation I have to make at the Management Conference in May.'

'Well, that's no problem, Naomi, it's all a matter of starting off by thinking of what doesn't work and then making sure you don't make the same mistakes as so many people do when they're faced with an audience. And you know what I consider the most important thing to remember?'

'*If I knew that, Uncle, I wouldn't be so worried! Tell me; I'm all ears ...*'

James raised his glass of beer.

'*Cheers! Here's to a successful presentation.*'

He smiled at her warmly. It would be rewarding to help her with this project.

'*The most important thing to bear in mind, whenever you are asked to make a presentation or a speech of any kind, is what the professionals call "the privilege of the platform". I'm sure you've heard some people get up on the stage and treat it as their right to have their say at the company meeting.*

'*It was your namesake, the American speaker Naomi Rhode, who first taught me that speaking from the platform is a privilege. For many years it was the title of her keynote speech, "The Privilege of the Platform".*

'*Some speakers are over-confident when they come on stage. They use all sorts of technical terminology and long words. In short, their arrogance separates them from their audience. What you want to do is get the audience to relate to you, to identify with the issues that you talk about.*'

James took another sip of his beer:

'*In your mind, what makes a really bad presentation? Is it the tone of voice, the fact that you can't hear, or the confusing PowerPoint slides? If you've ever wanted to get up and walk out, what was the single main factor that made you feel like that?*'

Naomi paused for a moment and then smiled:

'*Oh, dear! I suppose it's that feeling of "What am I doing here?" You must know what I mean. There's someone up on stage; usually a man behaving like Daddy did when I was a teenager and he wanted to know if I'd done all my homework. He's standing up there lecturing me and it's not even about something that is relevant to me – nor to most of the audience, I should imagine.*'

21

James's face lit up.

'That's exactly it, Naomitik. The speaker has been granted the privilege of the platform and he is simply abusing it. You must start off by recognizing the privilege and respecting your audience. If you respect them, they'll respect you.'

'But surely the speaker has to come on stage with some sort of authority. It's no good starting off by apologizing for being there, is it?'

'No, of course not, but they are – as they say – giving you the stage. Don't forget that. When you walk on, you claim the stage, you let them settle. Don't expect a standing ovation, but do realize that they respect you for being there and want you to show the confidence to reflect that in the way you begin.

'But we're racing ahead. I wanted to start by letting you get the feel of what I see as the essential context for any presentation.

'Now, let's go back for a moment and look at the content of what you're going to say. It's the financial slot, and there's a very logical structure, which I am sure you can tell me without any difficulty.'

Naomi reached for her notes, then had second thoughts and decided she knew what she wanted to say to her uncle.

'The essence of my contribution is to tell everyone what we did last year, where we are today and where we want to be in a year's time.'

James looked at Naomi with anticipation.

'And … is that it? Is that the whole presentation?'

Naomi looked puzzled.

'I'm not sure. What else should I be saying?'

'Well, Naomitik, if that's the structure of your presentation, then what have you told them that they don't already know?

'*They've all seen the results, they know where the company is today and they probably have a pretty good idea that the management team are going to be asking for more of the good stuff and less of the bad stuff in the coming twelve months. If that's all you're going to say then they've every right to sit there feeling bored.*'

James continued:

'*If that's it, what have they learned? Why should they waste their time listening to what they already know, when they could be in the bar networking with colleagues?*'

Naomi was surprised at James's suggestion that the sales force (*especially* the sales force) might spend their time better boozing in the bar with their mates than listening to the management team talking about the company and its business.

'*Really, Uncle, that's awful! We all know that the sales force like to come to these events to drink as much as they can when the company is paying. It's terrible to suggest that's an important part of the event.*'

James held his ground and argued back:

'*Two things, Naomitik. Firstly, one of the biggest benefits of any event that brings the team together is the informal team-building that takes place simply by being part of a larger group than they normally meet in the office.*

'*Secondly, everything that happens in the plenary sessions should be relevant, useful and informative for everyone in the audience. It should tell them what's going on and what they should do about it. I'll come back to what I said a moment ago. You've talked about your three headings:*

Where we've come from.

Where we are now.

Where we're going next.

'What you're doing in your presentation is moving the audience from point A to point B. That's your purpose; it's a journey. I said you'd missed something and I would have thought it would be obvious. Come on! You're too intelligent not to see what I'm driving at.'

Naomi reflected on the metaphor that James had been using: the idea of the journey from where the company had been to where it was headed. Suddenly it dawned on her.

'You're saying I should be telling them what it will take to get us there, aren't you? But that's not my role. That's sales. Or manufacturing—'

James butted in:

'Or marketing. Or HR. Or R&D. You see, Naomi, everyone each has their own contribution to that journey. No department can stand back and say it's not their business. The future of the company is everyone's business, and every department should be talking about what needs to be done to move the company forward.

'You know what the safety officers always say: "Health and Safety is everyone's business." That doesn't apply to Health and Safety alone; it's everything in the company.

'A company is a nuclear unit with everyone making their unique, different but essential contribution to the end result. That's what differentiates the great companies from the ones that are just doing OK. That's how your boss Bradley got to where he is today, and my guess is that he won't be expecting a bare news report from you. He'll be expecting you to tell people what the finance department needs from them to take the company on to bigger things.

'But I'll tell you where you want to start. You need to get a big piece of paper and braindump everything that you could possibly mention in your presentation. Don't hold back. That's the point about braindumping: no holds barred, nothing too outrageous. Just get it all down, then when you've had some time to think

about it you can start sorting it into sections. I always used a mind-mapping programme – there are plenty of good free versions available on the web; I'm sure you'll find one.'

Naomi thought for a moment and realized that her presentation was going to be much more dynamic than she had initially envisaged.

Uncle James was right. It wasn't enough to give a report; she had an obligation to tell the audience what was expected of them. There were some things that they needed to do differently, and there were other areas in which they needed to do different things from what they had been doing up to now. There were certainly areas in which they would have to start thinking differently, even if they wouldn't be personally involved in specific actions in those areas.

It was all about change, always about change, just like a garden growing and always needing something doing. Which reminded her about the weeding, and dead-heading the roses. She would have been doing that now if … she realized her mind was wandering and pulled herself back.

'This is a great start, James. But give me some general tips, just so I can start thinking about how I can make it interesting. Let me buy you dinner. It's the least I can do.'

'My dear Naomitik, that would be delightful. It's so rewarding when children become adults and start to treat their elderly relative.'

'Uncle James! I could never think of you as elderly. For goodness sake! Your twins are only just leaving university.'

'But I do like the thought of you buying me dinner. Just let me treat you to the wine. They have some jolly good Burgundy here at the Station.'

Naomi and James continued their talk through dinner. He shared his experience in explaining some of the basics of how to make a structure engaging and interesting, and Naomi filled two pages with notes and ideas to take back with her. By the time she took the train home later that evening she had a clear idea of how she could put her message across. She started to think about marshalling the key points into an entertaining story.

Summary

Every presentation involves four elements:

1. The Proposer.
2. The Sponsor.
3. The Issue.
4. The Message.

The reputation or perceived credibility of any one of these elements can influence that of the other elements.

In the ideal scenario, a good presentation by the Proposer will put both the Sponsor and the Issue in a good light, with the result that the audience responds well to the Message, which is a call for Action – a plea for change.

In every situation, the purpose of a presentation or speech is to change the mindset of the audience. In simple terms, a presentation asks people either:

To think differently, or

To act differently

3

Making it relevant

The WIIFY factor

The renowned American speechwriter, Jerry Weissman, talks about the WIIFY factor, an acronym for 'What's In It For You?'

Whenever you have the task of speaking out, the audience will be sitting there, just as Naomi is learning from James, thinking: 'What's in it for me?'

As a speaker, you should be constantly focusing your message on the fact that the audience are all sitting there, thinking: 'What's in it for me?'

Understand this, and you'll understand the nub of what makes a bad presentation – the irrelevance of the content to the audience.

Naomi saw this when James explained that it was simply not enough to deliver a presentation of the facts. You have to deliver an interpretation and, more importantly, you have to tell the audience what you expect of them, what they have to do to move from A to B.

This is the journey – from thinking and acting the way they do at present, to thinking and acting differently in the future. This may mean actual physical changes in what they do, or a shift in their opinion and thinking about an issue.

'So, I'm listening. Now, what's in it for me?'

Facts by themselves are raw information. You live in the twenty-first century, when IT (information technology) has created the potential for all the basic management information to be made readily available to whatever audience you choose, through channels such as a company or private institutional intranet, as well as the traditional methods like newsletters and printed bulletins.

The essential communication function is interpreting this raw information into practical, relevant knowledge so that people can easily understand *what's in it for them* and what they have to do to make it happen.

Every day, you have statistics transmitted to you through the media.

Sometimes you are left to put your own interpretation on that information, but more often the media will deliver the information with a particular slant or spin. In the case of the popular media, such as the press and television, this is often to emphasize some sensationalist angle or partisan cause. We know all too well that one person's lawless terrorist is another person's heroic freedom fighter.

On the financial level, identical information frequently brings opposing reactions. A hike in interest rates brings dismay to home-buyers who have to meet their mortgage payments, and pleasure to pensioners who have savings.

The secret of communication is not distributing *information*; it is giving people an appropriate *interpretation* of this information, an interpretation that is relevant to them.

From what you have just read, you can see that the interpretation will not be the same for every audience. But in an era of mass communications it is not always easy to differentiate and give the right message to the right audience. You have to put yourself in the position of the audience and try to see things from their perspective.

Remember the golden rule – *what's in it for me?*

Corporate financial results are a good example of an area in which different audiences will want to hear different messages.

Employees will want to hear about job security and bonuses; shareholders will want to know about risk, profit and dividends; the public may want to know about products and prices; the community will be interested in corporate projects that might affect them.

So, what happens if you give them the bare facts?

The reality is that if you give the wrong messages to the wrong audience you can end up with the wrong result. Increased prices may be bad news for the consumer but good news for the investor, as long as the institutions think the market can accept price increases. Profit is still a dirty word for many people, even though the size of their pension will largely depend on the performance of the portfolio in which their pension is invested.

Grunt will have to think carefully about the issues he is going to highlight when it comes to the hustings for the election of a new leader of the tribe. He's already made his first mistake in not working out exactly who his audience will be.

The battle of the sexes

Tork met Grunt outside his cave to discuss a new piece of information.

'Hello, Grunt. I suppose you've heard about Wizpa and Chat?'

Wizpa and Chat were two women who had brought their families from the tribes beyond the hills, to join Tork and Grunt's people and make a new home with them on the mountain. They had introduced the new skills of fishing and cooking and had taught these to the womenfolk on the mountain, much to their delight.

'What about them?

'They've decided to stand.'

'Huh ...?'

'For election. Wizpa and Chat have decided that the leadership of the tribe has been too male-dominated and that women should be involved in decision-making.'

To say that Grunt was shocked would be an understatement. It was bad enough when these outsiders had introduced fish into their diet. Fish wasn't manly; it was fiddly and full of bones. Then these women had them taking the meat that Grunt had hunted and putting it in the fire. They called it 'cooking'. Grunt said that real men liked their meat juicy, something to get their teeth into, not dried up and falling apart.

And now, these women wanted to be in the Council of Elders. That was going too far. 'Whatever next!' he thought. Grunt didn't know where to begin.

'So, now they want to join the elders. I don't know, Tork, what on earth am I to say at the hustings tomorrow?'

'Look, Grunt, to start with you must think about your audience. Remember that half the tribe is made up of women. Then about two-thirds of the tribe come from either your or my people. The other third is made up of Chat and Wizpa's people, plus a few travellers who've settled here since we moved together.'

'So it's no good me thinking I can just tell them what a brilliant hunter I am and think that's enough?'

'It's not just that, Grunt. It's not about who you are and what a nice chap you are – it's about what these people are looking for in a leader.

'We've got to get our heads together and braindump some ideas about what people want, what's relevant to them, what they want changed and – equally importantly – what they want leaving just as it is.

'Once we've worked out what the issues are, we can start thinking about your ideas and your manifesto.'

Grunt's face broke into a broad grin.

'Gosh, a manifesto! I certainly never thought I'd have a manifesto. What is that? Is it my chain of office? I could have a manifesto made of mammoth teeth. That would be wicked, cool, mint, man!'

Tork heaved a sigh. What on earth had induced him to take on Grunt's PR as some sort of unpaid election agent?

'No, old chap, a manifesto is what you say you're going to do if you become leader. Like I say, we need to work out what people want, what's relevant to them, and then work out what different things you're going to do from what Alto did as leader.'

'Oh, I see. There's a lot to this business, isn't there?'

'Yes, Grunt, but don't worry. We'll get there.'

Grunt dreams of his moment of glory

So, what's the issue?

You've established that every presentation is designed to make changes, and that whatever you say has to be relevant to the audience. Now it's time to get down to work by establishing what the issues are.

You'll recall that **Issue** is one of the four elements of every presentation. It's not the action that you want the audience to take, but the *context* that leads to the action you will propose. In the earlier example, it was the plight of elderly people living alone; this was the existing situation that created the impetus for asking for volunteers to make home visits.

In Naomi's case, she had initially seen the issue as the financial report; while she was correct in identifying that as an important part of the presentation, it's not the **Issue**, it's the *background*.

Sometimes people skim over talking about the **Issue** and go straight to outlining the **Action**. Imagine what happens if a speaker does that, which was Grunt's first instinct when he tried to put together his notes for the hustings.

Grunt didn't like the thought of having to debate with two women, so he decided that he would go on the attack by setting out his manifesto from the start, as he explained to Tork:

> *'I've been thinking about this manifesto thingy, and I've decided how I'm going to start my speech next week, Tork. I'm going to be clear and not nervous; I'm going to tell them what I'm going to do so they all know where I stand. You really helped me straighten out my ideas, Tork, thank you. Listen to this.'*

Tork tried to raise an encouraging smile, but he was apprehensive about the direction that Grunt seemed to be intent on taking:

> *'Right, Grunt, let's hear it then.'*

Grunt drew himself up to his full height and fixed his eyes on the middle-distance:

> *'Men of the mountain tribe! If you choose to elect me as your leader, the women will no longer go off to the lake every morning to fish. The men will now take full responsibility for the meat and fish that we eat, leaving the women to attend to their work in the caves, looking after the children, preparing the food that we bring back and stitching the hides and furs into clothes.'*

Tork quickly interrupted:

> *'Hold on, Grunt, what did we say just now about the make-up of the tribe? It's more than half women. Don't you think you're getting off on the wrong foot?'*

Grunt thought for a moment:

'OK, I see. I'll start again. Men and women of the mountain tribe! If you choose to elect me as your leader, the women will no longer go off to the lake every morning to fish. The men will now take full responsibility for the meat and fish that we eat—'

Tork interrupted again:

'No, Grunt, you're still missing the point. Yes, of course you should greet everyone in your opening words. But you can't jump straight in with your big idea without giving people some background so that they understand the idea that you're proposing.

'You need to think how they would feel if Chat or Wizpa announced that they would be doing the hunting in future.'

'That's ridiculous, Tork. Women can't hunt – you know they can't.'

'But suppose they learned it as children, just like our boys. How would you feel if that was what they suggested?'

'I'd be furious, Tork, raving furious! I love my hunting and what's more I'm the best hunter in the tribe.'

'Hold on now, Grunt. I'd challenge that myself, and so would some of the younger men. Did you see the way young Chukka speared that mammoth, last time we went over the hills? That boy's got talent, I tell you.'

Grunt objected:

'It was a stroke of luck. Not like that time you and I did a double whammy, left and right, the angry young mammoth and the wild boar. D'you remember?'

And all thought of speech-making was forgotten as Tork and Grunt reminisced about their glorious times out hunting together.

Establishing the basic components

In order to hold the attention of the audience, you need to start by making an inclusive opening that shows you're talking to all of them.

This means **setting the scene**, and identifying the situation that needs to be addressed, in such a way that they understand how this affects them. When you do this, they can identify with the issue and see how it is relevant to them.

The second component is the **action** or process that is needed to make the necessary changes to create the move from the present situation to the ideal outcome.

The third component is the **target**, the objective, the encapsulation of where you want to be in the future, that is different from where you are now, and which is the result of following-through the solution.

Sometimes this will be a physical proposition, like the completion of a specific project. But it might just as well be something far vaguer or even spiritual, a theoretical ideal.

Martin Luther King's 'I have a dream ...' is an example of something that is broad and visionary. On the other hand, the presentation of proposals for the completion of the London 2012 Olympics project would be an objective that is ultra-specific.

So, there are three distinct components to the structure of a speech:

1. The context and consequent issue.
2. The solution and action.
3. The ideal outcome.

Aristotle's Rule of Three

Any presentation should be a kind of theatre. It's telling a story: you are leading the audience from A, where they were, to B, where you want them to be in the future. This is like the process in a three-act play.

It is widely accepted that the first person to think of a performance in terms of three 'acts' was the Greek philosopher and writer Aristotle in the fourth century BC. He is generally credited with inventing the concept of the three-act play, dividing it simply into:

➤ Beginning

➤ Middle

➤ End

The Hollywood formula

Hollywood scriptwriters are taught Aristotle's *Rule of Three* as the basic formula for constructing a screenplay.

Think about almost any movie you've seen, and you'll be able to identify the way that the first part introduces the characters and explains the situation, the second is full of action, and in the third part we see the end result.

It's totally logical and almost painfully obvious when you think about it. You could think of it in terms of past, present and future; birth, life and death or even top, middle and bottom. However you slice it, you have three components, and they all follow that basic sequence of beginning, middle and end.

And yet, despite the fact that it's pretty obvious that so much of life can be split into these three sections, it's all too easy to overlook the logic, simplicity and effectiveness of this structure.

What gets interesting is that, if you're smart, you can play around with the order of these components so that you can, if you wish, start by painting a glowing picture of the outcome, rather than build up to it at the end. You'll see later how this works out, when you look at creating the structure of a presentation.

Naomi had the right idea, but hadn't developed it into action. You'll see what happens when she met up with Uncle James again to discuss her revised thoughts.

Starter, main course and dessert

James drove into the car park of the Rose and Crown, a smart inn a couple of miles from the offices of Amethyst Holdings.

Just as he was locking his car, Naomi pulled up in her bright yellow cabriolet, hitting a discreet beep on the horn to attract his attention. James greeted her warmly and together they made their way into the dining room and took their seats at a corner table.

> *'My treat today, Naomitik, after that delicious meal you bought me when you came up to see me. Mind you, better keep off the wine since you're working and we're both driving.'*

> *'Afraid so, Uncle James.'*

> *'Please, it's James!'*

Naomi dropped her voice to a whisper:

> *'Yes, James, but I wanted those eavesdroppers by the bar to know you're my uncle and not my sugar-daddy.'*

> *'Ha, now I'll take that as a compliment! Being a sugar-daddy is something I never aspired to.'*

> *'Come now, James. All that travelling and you're telling me ...'*

James stepped in swiftly.

> *'That, my dear lady, is what I am not doing. I'm not telling you ... Now, let's get down to business. Shall we order lunch before they get busy here, and then we can focus on what you've come up with so far?'*

James quickly chose the daily special and, while Naomi tussled to make up her mind, he browsed over the mind-map document that she handed him. Once they had both ordered and the waitress had relieved them of the menus and the neglected wine-list, Naomi smiled expectantly, waiting to hear what James's reaction might be.

He studied the sheet that she had handed him.

> *'Now you're getting somewhere. This is very promising – if that doesn't sound patronising.'*

> *'Of course not, so tell me how I should continue.'*

37

'You need to group all these random topics into groups of topics that more or less fit together. I call it "bundling". You've got Sales and Marketing as separate headings, but you could group those. And Purchasing, Warehousing and Distribution could also go together – although some companies would need to put Distribution under Sales. There are no hard and fast rules about this; it depends on your company organization.

'What we could usefully do, over the next hour or so, is to work out the various headings that your audience would find logical and see how we can lead them through while you tell your story.'

'Yes, James, I'm beginning to understand that it really is much more story-telling than reporting. I think I've latched on to the ideas of the audience looking for what's in it for them, and my need to inspire changes in their thinking and the way they do things.'

'Precisely. And here, for example, you've mentioned the fact that you're changing the bonus structure. My guess is that you'll need to set a clear context for that, so that when you announce the detail they'll know what to expect.'

'My thinking is that by the time they hear the detail, they'll be relieved to hear that the changes are not as harsh as they could be, given the strain on resources in the coming year.'

'Now you're getting the right idea. Let's go over the points you want to make about the new product range.'

James and Naomi continued, deep in discussion, over the next hour or so. It was clear that the best way to reach this stage in the development of the presentation had been to get all the topics out on the table and then rank them in importance and group them into logical headings.

That had meant taking a no holds barred approach to **braindumping** – which is the subject of the next chapter.

Summary

Every audience is sitting there thinking: *'What's in it for me?'* Consequently, any speech or presentation must be relevant to the audience:

Speakers must be inclusive in the way that they address the audience.

Speakers must project the issue in a way that the audience can relate to.

The audience must understand why a particular course of action is being proposed.

The speaker must describe the outcome in such a way that the audience understands, regardless of whether they find the outcome appealing.

Presentations are a type of theatre: they break down into a structure similar to a three-act play with a beginning, a middle and an end.

The essential components of a presentation are:

The context and consequent issue.

The solution and action.

The (ideal) outcome.

4

Dumping and bundling

Braindumping

Whatever kind of interaction you are facing – whether it's a presentation, a negotiation or an interview – it's good to start by braindumping.

This is a bit like sorting out a box full of clutter: you tip it all out on the table, sort it out, and then decide what to keep and what to throw away.

When you are braindumping a presentation, you list all the possible issues and areas that might affect or influence the proposition.

What's more, in all of these types of interaction, the thought at the back of your mind is to remember that the other people are thinking: '*What's in it for me*?' But this is not to say that you don't need to give them the full story. Just bear in mind what they will find interesting and – here's that word again – *relevant*.

Raj is the Account Executive at Red Balloon Advertising, with responsibility for the Amethyst account.

He has set up a meeting with his team to plan a presentation for Amethyst, to announce the launch of their new *Explorer* product range. Because of the long-standing relationship Red Balloon has with Amethyst, he has invited the client, in the form of Marketing Director Jacqui, to sit in on the session.

'I think most of you have met Jacqui, who has been Amethyst's Marketing Director for the past couple of years. We've always worked very closely with Amethyst so I decided to take the unusual step of inviting Jacqui to join us today. You've not all met before so let's quickly go round the table and introduce ourselves.'

Jacqui spoke first, and then the Red Balloon team made their introductions. Raj had brought in all eight members of the team who worked in the agency, but since a couple were recently recruited trainees and a couple of others had only a fleeting knowledge of Amethyst, he started with some background.

'Let me start by giving you the history. Amethyst manufacture luggage. They are best known for the top quality Club Class line that they produce, which is branded in conjunction with Provincial Black – Provincial Bank's top prestige charge card.

'Amethyst has been aware for some time that the market has changed. More people are travelling by air and not expecting their luggage to last for more than a few holidays.

'They are buying cheap suitcases from discount stores, and increasingly from special promotions at supermarkets. The department stores have been the main distribution channel for Amethyst in the past, and these traditional outlets are disgruntled at seeing their market share declining.

'Amethyst have committed themselves with their overseas suppliers for volume production of a new product line, Amethyst Explorer, based on their market research. Red Balloon has been given the task of planning a major trade launch to coincide with the Travel Goods Show in Las Vegas in the first week of March.

'The proposal is that, in addition to taking a booth at the exhibition, Amethyst will be hosting a cocktail party on the second evening of the show, at which Jacqui will make a 15-minute presentation to all their top customers from the USA and Europe.

'Have I got that right, Jacqui?'

Jacqui smiled:

'Absolutely, Raj. We know there is a huge market for a quality range in the budget market. Our research shows that people get annoyed with suitcases that rip or fall apart and that they are looking for something that offers affordable quality. You worked with us on some of the research, Raj, so you'll remember the findings, I'm sure.'

Jacqui handed back to Raj, who continued:

'It was interesting, Jacqui. As you say, there's a market out there, taking up to five long weekends a year in addition to at least one main holiday. They want luggage that suits this lifestyle.

'Now, the new Explorer range has a number of features. All the models have a lightweight metal frame and an injection-moulded body. The back of the smaller models has a zip section that conceals shoulder straps so that the luggage can be carried as a back-pack. The target market goes from gap year students, to families, to businessmen – so that's pretty broad.

'I want to start with a braindumping session, on anything that you associate with the Amethyst range in general, and Amethyst Explorer in particular. I'll jot your words down on this interactive whiteboard panel and they'll come up on the screen. It saves me getting up and writing on the old whiteboard and easel.'

Walter, the creative head of the agency started off:

'Fashion. Number one attribute: luggage is a personal accessory so fashion is a must.'

Immediately, an argument started between Malaika, his assistant, and Walter himself:

'What do you mean, Walter? I can't see that fashion is important for luggage! All people want is something strong, durable and lightweight.'

Walter responded immediately:

> *'Oh, come on now Mal! Fashion is everywhere today. The days when you could sell something just because it was durable and whatever are gone; that's very twentieth century. No, on second thoughts, positively nineteenth century!'*

Raj interrupted:

> *'Look, I'm not going to agree or disagree with either of you. The whole point of braindumping is that we get what everyone thinks. Nothing is right or wrong. There are no bad or irrelevant contributions.*
>
> *'The thing about mass marketing is that there will be different people looking for different things in any product. We should have a pretty good cross-section of ideas around the table, so don't hold back and let's get everything up on the board.*
>
> *'Now – anyone want to propose something really controversial? How about fragrance? I love the smell of leather.'*

Malaika sniggered:

> *'Let's keep your private life out of this, Raj.*
>
> *'Anyway, this luggage is metal, nylon, fibreglass and fabric. No leather; not even latex, Raj, if that's what you fancy instead of leather.'*

Before Raj could reply to her barefaced cheek, Mal continued:

> *'OK, then, I'll stick with my three: strong, durable and lightweight.'*

No holds barred

Braindumping is a blue-sky activity. Nothing is too whacky, nothing too mundane, because the group represents different opinions and attitudes.

It's important to capture different people's different ideas.

You must put a time-limit on braindumping, because without any rules or limits it can go off on a tangent. Depending on the size of the group, 10–15 minutes is about right.

If you're writing your presentation by yourself, without the benefit of having input from a team of colleagues, braindumping on your own is a great way to start. Just don't let yourself get stuck: scribble away for 5–10 minutes, then put it to one side. Come back to it after you've spent some time working on another task. That way you'll find that you don't suffer from too much of a creative blockage and will come up with additional ideas when you pick up the list again.

Here's what Raj's team came up with when they braindumped: '*Luggage*, *Amethyst*, and *Amethyst Explorer*':

strong	compartments for shoes	business trips	gap year students
durable		airlines	
lightweight	travel	jet-lag	cityscapes
fashion	holidays	passport	glamour
bright	weekends	currency	family
expensive	adventurous	transfers	beach
discounted	exotic	hotels	sunshine
versatile	romantic	villas	sunburn
reputable	exciting	holiday rep	sun tan lotion
secure	long-haul	language	clubbing
easy wheels	driving	currency	hangover
straps inside	airport	carousel	credit cards
smart	check-in	customs officers	backache

They stopped at backache.

This was the suggestion from the rather traditionalist company bookkeeper who, they then discovered, had inherited his father's suitcases. He saw no point in spending good money on new ones with built-in wheels when he only used suitcases twice a year.

At this point, the group burst into roars of laughter and Raj called for a break to replenish the coffee.

What happened in this session is typical of any braindumping. The list starts to go off at a tangent. So, while they started on luggage with words like Malaika's first contribution, 'strong, durable and lightweight', they gradually moved into 'travel, holidays' and finally 'hangovers and credit cards'. The latter two have no direct connection with luggage but are, at least for this group of advertising people, associated with holidays.

There's always some scope for moving away from direct association and coming at the subject from an angle; companies do it all the time, especially in consumer advertising campaigns. However, on this occasion Red Balloon were looking for the trade angle in particular.

Raj started a second list, this time thinking specifically in terms of what the trade might already associate with Amethyst – and what they might, from their experience of Amethyst's current image, bring the trade to associate with Amethyst Explorer.

This produced a somewhat different list of key words:

Quality	Good margin	Sales support – consumers
High price (Business Class)	Design	
Fashion	Reliable	Prompt delivery
Value (Explorer)	Warranty/ guarantee	Consumer promotions
Reputation	Service to retailers	PR coverage
Style	Sales support – trade	Staff training/literature

The first observation is that a broad diversity of images is thrown up by all of these words.

The next step was to sort these into categories. So, Raj had the team work with him to decide how to group the various words, while he sketched out the result on the whiteboard.

Raj finished drawing out the mind-map on the whiteboard and then turned to the team:

> 'OK. That's a picture of what comes to mind for us when we think about the company, its products and its distribution channels.

> 'Now, we can see that the company has a great reputation, albeit for their top-end product range. They also have excellent standing as a trade supplier.

> 'The question is – what do we want to say to them in this 15-minute presentation?'

Walter started, circling some of the key words on the board:

> 'What we have here is a company with a high-class, prestige image. We then have a lot of fun and pleasure associated with the consumer attitude to luggage – holidays, family fun, and romance. What we have to do is identify the Explorer range with all those warm and comfortable emotions, and then splice that onto the excellent reputation they have as a reliable trade supplier.'

Once again, Malaika sparred with her boss:

> 'I disagree. If we're not careful, the Amethyst market will shift straight over to the Explorer range, and the retailers will be doing less turnover even if they sell more units. This looks to me like a disaster waiting to happen. If we're not careful, then the wrong campaign could destroy their present high-end business.'

Jacqui intervened:

> 'If I may come in here for a moment, Raj, I think both viewpoints are valid. Where I think you need to be very careful is in mixing the messages.

> 'The consumers need to be sold this as a brand with a clear identity, that is distinctly different from Club Class. On the other

hand, for the trade, we want to build on all that strong loyalty that you can see on the right hand side of the board.'

Raj took the floor again:

'Thanks, Jacqui.'

Then he turned to Malaika and Walter.

'Walter, I admire your creativity, and Malaika, we hired you because you were prepared to speak out. But we've got to get the balance right.

'We want to show the trade how we will appeal to the public, but at the same time we want Amethyst to come from the strength of their supplier relationship with the distribution channels, to home-in on a solid market opportunity.'

Raj turned and gestured to the mind-map on the whiteboard.

'We want to communicate the size of the opportunity; and we want to get the buyers thinking of this as a significant segmentation of the market. It's not just the launch of a new product; it's diversification into a new product area.

'For the public, the nub of the message is that it's affordable and it's Amethyst; for the trade it's a complete new business from Amethyst, their trusted and reputable supplier.'

Walter sighed and hit his palm against his brow. He spoke wearily and with heavy overtones of sarcasm:

'That's waffle, Raj! What's worrying the trade is that they're not getting their slice of the cake; it's going instead to discount stores, supermarkets, special promotions. Right now what you're saying is as boring as a Government White Paper.'

Raj smiled broadly:

'And that, dear Walter, is why you are Creative Director. Your job is to turn our boring mundane concept into a riveting 15-minute presentation. Now, let's start working on some ideas while we're all together here, so we don't get off-track ...'

47

Raj and Walter eventually reconciled their squabble. You will see what they came up with, later in the book, when you start to consider how to illustrate your presentation.

Mixed messages

What became clear in this example is the need to work out the right message for the right audience.

The braindumping clearly showed that the consumer message would be very different from the trade message. It was then left to Walter to find a way of developing a strong brand identity that would work for both trade and consumers, and then to stamp this clearly on the trade presentation.

Remember what you learned in Chapter Two: there are four components in any presentation. In this one which Jacqui will deliver in Las Vegas, her personality and dynamism will help project the company in a very favourable light. That sets the context for her analysis of the issue, much of which will focus on the opportunity created by the market segmentation.

Then there's the call for action: the promotion of the Explorer range as the response to the market opportunity and an invitation for the trade to partner with Amethyst in exploiting this opportunity.

Summary

To create the content, whether you are working alone or in a team, start with a braindumping session:

> There are no right or wrong contributions to braindumping.

Once everything is jotted down, start to group the ideas so that you have bundles of words and concepts that fit together under headings that can form sections and sub-sections of your presentation.

The next challenge is to develop a storyline, a structure, that will lead the audience, and ... everyone loves a good story.

5

Planning the structure

In the beginning ...

A story, like a play, follows Aristotle's rule: it has a beginning, a middle and an end.

Most books, plays and movies follow this sequence because the story they are telling evolves chronologically. Once in a while they will break the rules and intersperse the story with flashbacks, or glimpses of the future, but by and large Aristotle's rule is applied chronologically, moving the reader, audience or viewer from A to B so that at the end they either act or think differently.

When you're making a speech or presentation, you are telling a story and moving your audience from A to B.

But while there is a time element in the sense that the objective is to make your audience think or act differently *after* your presentation, from the way they did *before* your presentation, you don't have to tell your story in the same restrictive way.

In fact, you can put the three elements of your story into any order you like, and achieve different effects and a different impact according to which way you choose to do it. Consider how Naomi might structure her financial presentation.

Most Finance Directors stick to the well-worn chronological formula:

That's where we were/what we spent/what we earned last year. (past)

This is our financial position today. (present)

This is what we plan to spend/earn next year – and this will be the result. (future)

Now look at some alternative options:

This is where we want to be. (future)

This is where we've come from. (past)

This is where we're starting. (present)

Alternatively:

This is where we're starting. (present)

This is where we've come from. (past)

This is where we want to be. (future)

And so forth.

In total, there are six different ways that Naomi could shuffle the three chronological elements of her presentation to create a different structure. Each has its merits.

Don't just restrict yourself to the logical sequence of chronological order. Naomi's presentation has a strong chronological logic to it. This is because the finance function in the company is looking at the progression of results through a time-frame.

There are probably other structures she might choose to adopt, but basing it on past, present and future (in whatever order) works well.

That said, the majority of speeches and presentations are not naturally chronological.

Speeches, presentations and weddings

If you are making a Best Man's speech at a wedding, you could adopt the chronological structure and look back at the lives of the two individuals since their childhood, then the present day, and finally their life together in the future.

But there are many other approaches you could use. For example, you could devote one section to the groom's life as a bachelor, another section to the bride's single life and then talk about them as a couple.

Let's imagine that you're making the charity presentation described earlier, about the need for volunteers to visit old people who live alone. Your sections would be very different.

You might start by describing the general work of the charity and its history, then talk about the specific problems of elderly people living alone, and then contrast that with the lives of most people living with friends or family, finally linking this to an appeal for volunteers to devote some of their free time to visiting.

If you are Raj, preparing the trade presentation for the launch party at an international trade show, you might start by talking about the exciting new market opportunity; you could then contrast this with the traditional market, emphasizing Amethyst's reputation and strength in this market. Finally, you could talk about the new product range, linking it back to both the market opportunity and the reputation of Amethyst.

In fact, Walter has different ideas, as you'll find out later.

All three of these structures embody three key sections, which form the beginning, middle and end of the presentation, conforming to Aristotle's Rule of Three – but is there a hard-and-fast mandatory sequence? No!

The presenter is free to deliver the three sections in any order, provided that he makes the opening section an effective **Beginning**, expands on the story in the **Middle** section, and draws the arguments together in the final section to make effective **End**.

The sequence is what you choose to make it. But before you consider the implications of that statement, and see the fun you can have moving the three sections around to create a different impact and emphasis, take a look first at this mystical 'Rule of Three'.

Furniture, waltzes, biology and Goldilocks

When some speakers are planning a speech, they like the image of a three legged stool, representing the three points they plan to communicate.

With three legs, a stool is always perfectly stable, even if the legs are not all exactly the same length. If the stool has four legs there is a danger of a wobble, and if it has any more than four it becomes increasingly difficult to create something that is solid and stable.

The Rule of Three works for three-legged stools, and it works just as well for speeches and presentations.

Other speakers are more philosophical and think in terms of natural order. They visualize a speech in terms of the fundamentals of existence: birth, life and death. Or sowing the seeds, nurturing plants and harvesting the crop.

Personally, I'm a bit of a romantic: I think in terms of sounds and music. The waltz has a natural rhythm of three beats to the bar; the wolf-whistle is based around a middle note with notes above and below it, making it a sequence of three tones.

The example you are going to study in a moment is the children's story of Goldilocks and the Three Bears. You'll recall that not only are there three bears in the story, but furthermore there are three examples in the story each of which is a group of three.

The Rule of Three works. It's all around us. It's here, there and everywhere – which is yet one more example.

Look up 'Rule of Three' in Wikipedia, and you'll find more: from the sociological basis for decision-making, to positioning the subject matter when you are framing a photograph in the viewfinder. It doesn't matter which example works as a reminder for you. Just remember that it works in many aspects of life and it works particularly well when you are drafting any sort of speech or presentation. No matter how much or how little you want to communicate, condense what you want to say into three sections. Remember Julius Caesar and the three-word statement he wrote in a report to

Rome in 47 BC after invading Britain, and which everyone can probably remember from schooldays. *Veni, vidi, vici* – I came, I saw, I conquered.

The Rule of Three has a rhythm to it, it is logical and it is very powerful.

The Goldilocks Principle

When I started to research this idea I, like the bears returning to the cottage, found to my horror that *someone had been there before me.* There is another 'Goldilocks Principle'.

Astronomers have used this term in relation to the differences between our three adjacent planets, on the basis that, like the bowls of porridge in the Goldilocks story, Venus is too *hot*, Mars is too *cold*, but Earth is *just right*.

But this book isn't talking about presentations in terms of being hot, cold or just right. You will now see a broader view as you examine the persistent use of the Rule of Three, firstly throughout the well-known children's story, and then as you explore it as a tool for constructing a speech.

There are many versions of this well-known children's fairy story.

Some depict Goldilocks as being wayward and disobedient, others paint an aggressive and angry picture of the bears. While most versions describe the food on the cottage table as porridge, others say it was soup. These details may reflect local culture or the writer's desire to make a particular moral point about behaviour and obedience – but the structure is always identical.

In examining the story, you are looking at the structure rather than the thread of the story. Because Goldilocks offers a perfect example, not only of how to tell a story, but also of how to construct a powerful and effective presentation.

To start with, here is a typical version of the tale.

The story of Goldilocks and the Three Bears

Once upon a time, there was a little girl named Goldilocks. She went for a walk in the forest. Pretty soon, she came upon a house. She knocked and, when no one answered, she walked right in.

At the table in the kitchen, there were three bowls of porridge. Goldilocks was hungry. She tasted the porridge from the first bowl.

'*This porridge is too hot*!' she exclaimed, so she tasted the porridge from the second bowl.

'*This porridge is too cold*!' she said, so she tasted the last bowl of porridge.

'*Ahhh, this porridge is just right*!' she said happily, and she ate it all up.

After she'd tasted the three bears' breakfasts she decided she was feeling a little tired. So, she walked into the living room where she saw three chairs. Goldilocks sat in the first chair to rest her feet.

'*This chair is too big*!' she exclaimed, so she sat in the second chair.

'*This chair is too big, too*!' she whined, so she tried the last and smallest chair.

'*Ahhh, this chair is just right*!' she sighed.

But just as she settled down into the chair to rest, it broke into pieces! Goldilocks was very tired by this time, so she went upstairs to the bedroom. She lay down in the first bed, but it was too hard. Then she lay in the second bed, but it was too soft. Then she lay down in the third bed and it felt just right. Goldilocks fell fast asleep.

While she was sleeping, the three bears came home.

'*Someone's been eating my porridge*,' growled the Papa bear.

'*Someone's been eating my porridge*,' said the Mama bear.

'*Someone's been eating my porridge and they ate it all up*!' cried the Baby bear.

'*Someone's been sitting in my chair,*' growled the Papa bear.

'*Someone's been sitting in my chair,*' said the Mama bear.

'*Someone's been sitting in my chair and they've broken it all to pieces*!' cried the Baby bear.

They decided to look around some more. When they got upstairs to the bedroom, Papa bear growled:

'*Someone's been sleeping in my bed.*'

'*Someone's been sleeping in my bed, too,*' said the Mama bear.

'*Someone's been sleeping in my bed and she's still there*!' exclaimed the Baby bear.

Just then, Goldilocks woke up and saw the three bears. She screamed:

'*Help*!'

And she jumped up and ran out of the room. Goldilocks ran down the stairs, opened the door, and ran away into the forest. And she never returned to the home of the three bears.

Analysing the fairy story

Without yet going into the detail of trying to see the relevance to speech-writing, you can study the story and analyse its content and structure.

Firstly, look at the characters.

There are three bears, and each is contrasted in turn with the central personality of Goldilocks. The bears are characterized as the Papa, the Mama and the Baby. Goldilocks rejects the extremes that are portrayed by the two parent figures, but easily identifies with Baby Bear.

55

Then, consider the scenarios.

There are three situations that Goldilocks experiences: tasting the bowls of porridge, sitting on the chairs and lying on the beds. Goldilocks approaches each situation and finds two extremes – *too hot/too cold* or *too hard/too soft* and one acceptable compromise or midpoint *just right*.

Now, look at the outcomes.

In each scenario, there are two assessments or comparisons followed by a third one. This third one then leads to a specific outcome – she eats all the porridge, she breaks the chair, and then she falls asleep in the bed.

A further point about the outcomes is that the first scenario has a positive outcome – she happily eats up all the last bowl of porridge. The second scenario has a negative outcome –she breaks the chair and presumably lands on the floor with a painful bump.

It's a one-all score as we come to the final scenario, and the listener is waiting to see whether this will be a good or a bad outcome. In true dramatic style, it's a bit of both – and yet another Rule of Three! Goldilocks falls into a happy sleep (good outcome), only to be disturbed when the bears come home (bad outcome), but she escapes and runs off home, having a learned a lesson about respecting other people's privacy (good outcome).

Aristotle meets Goldilocks ...

Aristotle's Rule of Three permeates the Goldilocks story with constant groups of three – or triads, as they are sometimes called.

It won't be long before you find yourself listening to someone speaking and identifying triads.

As you listen carefully, you'll hear opportunities missed when a politician rambles on to deliver four or five points, or cuts his flow short by listing only two.

... and Goldilocks meets Beethoven

What you can also see from Goldilocks is that there is a real rhythm to using triads, such that the listener develops an anticipation that holds his or her attention.

This satisfying 'beat' is sometimes then underlined when the speaker adds a fourth and final point or conclusion, by way of a punchline.

I call this the '**Beethoven Imperative**' because it echoes the famous opening bars of Beethoven's Fifth Symphony. This starts with two musical motifs of four notes, each consisting of three quavers followed by a paused minim.

For those not familiar with musical terms, it goes: Dee-dee-dee ... Dum; Daa-daa-daa ... Dom.

Or for those who know their notes, G-G-G-E flat; F-F-F-D!

It is powerful, both musically and in a speech – but, if you use it too much, you do run the risk of becoming boringly repetitive.

In the story of Goldilocks and the Three Bears you can observe this flow of one, two, three and a punchline:

➤ Too hot, too cold, just right – she eats it all up
➤ Too big, still too big, just right – she settles down and breaks the chair
➤ Too hard, too soft, just right – she falls asleep

And this rhythm is echoed exactly with the reactions of the bears on their return:

➤ Someone's been eating my porridge
➤ Someone's been eating my porridge
➤ Someone's been eating my porridge

Followed by Baby Bear's punchline:

➤ ... and they ate it all up!

There are similar examples from the Bears' reactions for the chairs and the beds; each time it's one, two, three and then the punchline.

Best Man – worst nightmare!

Many men dread being approached by their best friend and asked to act as Best Man at his wedding.

The Best Man is a ritual role, dating back to the days when the groom's close friend was responsible for defending the groom against raiding parties from the bride's village wanting to steal back their lost daughter.

These days there is less open violence – unless the stag night party becomes totally out of hand.

There are still specific ritual roles that the Best Man is expected to perform, and certain responsibilities that are totally his. He takes charge of many of the arrangements, including hire of formal clothing and limousine transport, and he looks after critical documents such as tickets and passports for the honeymoon. The Best Man also holds the wedding rings until the appropriate moment in the ceremony.

However, the one role that seems to terrify even the most bold and outgoing Best Man is the prospect of the speech that he is required to make.

The function of the speech is to propose a toast to the health and happiness of the bride and groom.

Traditionally, this is done by reflecting humorously on the lives of the couple since childhood, incorporating amusing and often embarrassing stories about them, and finally eulogizing about their future.

Using the Goldilocks Principle, there are a number of possible approaches, each of which uses the triad process.

The one we suggested earlier was to structure the speech around the groom, the bride and the couple. Another option would be to follow the classical chronological order and talk about past, present and future.

Here is another example of how a completely different theme – sport – can be incorporated to create a theme that runs through an entertaining speech.

This is the framework of the speech that was made at the wedding of Amethyst's Marketing Director, Jacqui to Alan by the bridegroom's Best Man, Han. You will see from his notes how this fits into the structure you have been studying in the fairytale.

Han's Best Man's speech for Alan's wedding

➢ Introduction ➢ Set the scene	➢ Welcome, introduce self	➢ Joke to link ➢ Almost 300,000 weddings in UK every year – please check you're at the right one
➢ Alan's childhood	1. Babyhood story about his addiction to eating the dog's food – probably why he loves donner kebabs today 2. His time as a Cub Scout – comment on his Home Help badge and read out requirements: boil kettle, lay table, do washing-up (list all the tasks) ➢ Joke how Jacqui will appreciate that 3. How we first met playing football for the under-11 side on Saturday mornings	➢ Joke to link to School ➢ I remember the first time Alan 'scored' – he was 9 and I was 10 … etc ➢ Link to secondary school
➢ Alan's teenage years	1. How he chose to do Biology because he expected there would be course work. But, like Biology examinations, it wasn't quite what he expected 2. Other school interests – make remarks about useful DIY skills ➢ Produce the wobbly pot-stand he made for his mother and the non-matching bookends he made for his dad 3. Still playing football, and dreaming of being a star, but only star was the one on his badge at his Saturday job at McDonald's. All the girls knew that size was important, which is why, every Saturday, they wanted to get their hands on Alan's Big Mac	➢ Joke to link to adult ➢ Every girl he dated he tried to teach the off-side rule, and every girl he dated tried to teach him the off-limits rule ➢ I don't think either he or the girls ever quite understood …

59

➤ Alan's adult years	1. We won't labour over Alan's years at university – he certainly didn't. Talk about various activities 2. His questionable taste in fashion ➤ Produce floral shirt and comment (!) 3. Football became an excuse to travel – as on the team trip to Belgium (tell story about Café du Gare)	
	1. Graduated and joined Thimbletons accountants and rapidly promoted and posted overseas. 2. Possible joke about getting rid of him? 3. Too hot over there to play football, so joined the tennis club and won the President's trophy	
	1. Came back to London office 2. Bought a flat in Wimbledon with all the money he made overseas and … 3. … joined the tennis club	➤ Link to Jacqui 1. Then they met 2. She fell for his forehand 3. It wasn't deuce – it was love all – was this a championship match?

➤ Jacqui as an infant	1. Comment on Jacqui's early tennis prowess
	   ➤ Produce child's tennis racquet and tennis dress
	2. Unlike Alan, Jacqui was a fairy
	   ➤ Produce her childhood fairy party dress
	   ➤ With fairy wand and wings
	3. While Alan was a Cub Scout, Jacqui was busy with the Brownies. He'll be pleased to know she earned her needlework and First Aid badges, though he may find that her knitter badge might be rather embarrassing
	   ➤ Produce jumper she knitted
		➤ Joke to link
		➤ Given Alan's questionable taste in fashion, maybe we can already see that they were clearly made for each other

➤ Jacqui as a teenager	1. I'm sure Jacqui's beginning to wonder what I might have unearthed about her teenage years, but I've decided that discretion is the better part of valour. It would be remiss of me not to talk about her more laudable achievements. Consistently raised large sums of money for Cancer Research – sponsored walks and school concerts etc
	2. Saturdays were spent perusing the shops with her gang, though she probably never remembers Alan's first words to her …
	  ➤ 'Do you want fries with that?'
	  ➤ Many years would pass before she started thinking about Alan's Big Mac
	3. It was no surprise to her parents, David and Maureen, when she became first a Prefect and then Head Girl. She left school a star pupil and – yes, I can see you're ahead of me – in the county youth tennis team
		➤ Joke to link
		➤ Was she about to meet the ball-boy of her dreams?
		➤ Not yet; Jacqui was about to discover the delights of Australia and the lure of the surf …

➤ Jacqui as an adult	1. Created successful marketing career in Australia 2. Returned to UK 3 years ago and landed an excellent job 3. Rented a flat just a mile from where Alan had bought a flat in Wimbledon and – yes – joined the tennis club!	➤ Joke to link 1. Was it time for mixed doubles? 2. Was there more to Wimbledon than tennis? 3. Would she fall for the way he bounced his balls before service?

➤ Alan and Jacqui	1. It was tennis that brought them together and there's a magic about tennis – wizards and witches
	  ➤ Look at Goran – even he's a witch (Ivanisević)
	    … oh, please yourselves!
	2. They courted on the courts and off the courts until finally they caught each other
	3. And so, ladies and gentlemen, that brings us all here together today to celebrate a tennis match
	1. May they long play doubles
	2. May the Almighty Umpire look kindly on their faults and
	3. May they always give the game of life their best shots
		➤ Closing remarks
		➤ Please be upstanding and raise your glasses to drink the enduring health and happiness of Jacqui and Alan

Benevolent triads – the 'Sudoku Structure'

Throughout this structure you can see how Han has used the Rule of Three not only by having a clear Beginning, Middle and End, but also – within each section – making just three topics each time, and using triads time and again to create a rhythm that his audience will feel and appreciate.

You have seen this in the Goldilocks Principle, but you could equally call it the 'Sudoku Structure' because you are building in threes, like the 3 x 3 x 3 grid of a Sudoku puzzle.

The body of Han's speech divides neatly into talking about Alan, talking about Jacqui, and finally talking about them as a couple.

It is also a gallant and chivalrous speech. There are many jokes at the groom's expense, making fun of his lack of fashion sense, his Saturday job at McDonald's and his time at university. (Note the triad in that sentence.)

When he talks about Jacqui, Han is more gentle. He talks about her charity work, her sporting triumphs and her successful career. (Yes, you're right, there's another triad!) This is also reflected in the timing of the speech, with more than half the time devoted to making fun of Alan.

When it comes to talking about the couple, he could have told stories about their time together. Instead, he chose to restrict himself to a few well-chosen words and lead straight into the toast.

The initial braindumping

One thing that will be immediately apparent to you is that Han had done his homework.

He clearly sat down with both sets of parents, and not only gleaned crucial information about the couple's individual childhood experiences, but has also borrowed useful props to illustrate his speech.

You will learn more about props in a later section, when you study the illustration and delivery of a presentation or speech.

It's easy to imagine Han, sitting down with the parents, armed with a blank sheet of paper, and listing anecdotes and other general pieces of background material. Many of these he would never use – but, like a great photographer, a good speaker is not known simply by the material he uses but by the volume of good material he discards.

You can never do too much background research on your topic; the secret is in bundling the different ideas into groups with a common thread, and then picking out which pieces to use and which to leave out.

Single facts are not as powerful as bundles. This is why it works well to list all the tasks that Alan had to complete to win his Home Help badge as a Cub Scout, rather than to mention just one or two.

As you read this, you can almost hear the audience's reaction, starting with a chuckle and then rising to an increasing volume of laughter. Assuming Han is smart, he will use the triad, and then the punchline. He might choose to say something like this:

While he was a Cub Scout, Alan won many badges. Some of them may prove useful in married life, others less so.

Alan won his Book Reader badge. Hmm ... not promising. He gained the badge for Communicator, that's better. But best of all was the badge for Home Help.

Note the triad – again. Han continues:

Let me tell you some of the things Alan had to do to win his Home help badge:

> *Lay a table*
> *Cook and serve a simple meal*
> *Wash up afterwards and show how to clean a saucepan or similar cooking utensils, cutlery, glassware, etc*

Jacqui, you have found your Superman! Look! He even had to convince the examiner that he could ...

> *Sew on a badge or button*

By the time I knew Alan [pause] *his expertise was in un-doing buttons, not sewing them back on*!

Han also makes some useful contrasts and comparisons between Alan and Jacqui.

Having discovered that Alan had been a Cub Scout, he clearly investigated whether Jacqui had been in the Girl Guiding movement. This enables him to make allusions to both, and when he starts to mention this in regards to Jacqui, his audience knows that there is a joke coming.

Knowing the audience and the culture of the occasion

It is a tradition of Best Man's speeches in the UK that the content is always a little risqué, without being smutty. Han steers a careful course through this and doesn't allow himself to be in any way indiscreet.

Most European audiences will expect to be treated in a way that they consider to be cosmopolitan and sophisticated, and they will have no problem if a speaker uses what might be described as 'adult humour'.

North American audiences are very different. They expect a more formal and respectful approach, and the humour is much more restrained and genteel.

Knowing the culture of the audience and being able to tailor a speech to suit the occasion is a skill well worth learning.

Etiquette and protocol are areas in which a stranger can make big errors by not observing the local culture. We've all heard stories of people making an embarrassing mistake, as a result of their ignorance of local culture. Frequently, this could have been avoided with a little astute research in advance.

There is a broad range of business travel guides available that will help you to observe the sort of foreign conventions that extend through all aspects of life in different countries; from removing shoes as you enter a home, and how to behave in mixed company, to how to handle the ritual of exchanging business cards.

When you are talking to an unfamiliar audience in a foreign country, you must be confident that you are not making any serious *faux pas.*

North American audiences are likely to be far more conservative than European ones, who will often consider Americans to be narrow-minded to the point of being puritanical.

It is especially important to take care with audiences that in the past would have been exclusively male but are now likely to be more evenly balanced between the sexes. Obviously, men addressing such a group need to be sensitive to the gender balance in the audience, and be both inclusive in their language and careful with the tone of their presentation.

At the same time, a male speaker in this situation will rapidly alienate his audience if he sounds the least bit patronizing.

It is less obvious, but equally important, that women addressing such a group should consider the feelings of the men in the audience, who may fear that their territory is being invaded and their value and contribution is being challenged. It harks back once again to the need to put yourself in the other person's shoes and constantly endeavour to see things from the other point of view.

When you're the senior woman facing a testosterone-charged male sales squad, you don't have to agree with their outlook and opinions – but you do have to try to understand it. You don't have to waver in your convictions; just remember that the people in the audience have given you the 'privilege of the platform' and you should respect their views, even if you don't hold the same views yourself.

And, guys, the same goes for you if you're faced with a predominantly female audience. Fail to follow this advice, and you may end up like British premier Tony Blair when he addressed the Annual Conference of the British Women's Institute in June 2000.

Some members of the audience felt that his speech was inappropriate to the occasion and too overtly political. They reacted by heckling and with a slow hand-clap – the traditional British way of expressing disapproval of an orator. Some delegates walked out of the conference and Blair cut his speech short. While his office said he did this to save time, it is more likely that this was a strategic response to the reception that the audience was giving him.

When you are developing the way you tell your story, so that the audience relate to the examples you use, you may well be tempted to use a sporting example. Since sport is a subject that many people seem to feel comfortable to discuss without hesitation, it is a popular way of structuring many types of presentation and speeches. Again, it's very much a matter of knowing and appreciating the culture of your audience.

However, sporting metaphors can be a minefield.

When a European speaker talks about 'football' to an American audience, there will be much confusion as to whether the speaker is referring to *NFL American football* (where players wear exaggeratedly bulky shoulder pads and protective helmets) or to *soccer*. While soccer is the dominant sport across all of Europe, it is more of a ladies' game in the States.

Similarly, the game known simply as *hockey* in Europe is called *field hockey* in the US, while *hockey* in North America is what we Europeans would call *ice hockey*.

And if you are going to talk about cricket, make sure you are in a country that has strong ties with the British Commonwealth if you wish to avoid blank uncomprehending faces looking back at you from the audience. On the other hand, if you are a North American speaking on the Indian sub-continent, a couple of knowledgeable allusions to the way that the cricket Test Matches are progressing will immediately earn you the admiration and approval of the audience.

In nearly all of the first section of this book, we have talked about only the *verbal* content of your presentation. Most business presentations would not be planned like that; they would start with a stack of PowerPoint slides.

Try doing it differently:

Think about the outcome you want to achieve.

Consider what you want people to think and do when you've finished speaking.

Work out how you are going to move your audience from where they are to where you want them to end up.

Plot out the story that you will tell.

Start by braindumping material and sifting through all the possible content that you could utilize.

The next step is to think about how to tell your story and keep the interest of your audience, which is what you will learn in the next chapter.

As for PowerPoint, you'll be considering how to illustrate your story vividly and with impact when you move on to Section Two.

Get the words right, then add the right visual support, and any anxiety and stagefright will be greatly diminished.

Summary

Aristotle meets Hollywood

As you learned in an earlier chapter, the formula that Hollywood adapted from Aristotle's original structure establishes three sections:

1. The context and consequent issue.
2. The solution and action.
3. The (ideal) outcome.

When you consider the structure of your presentation or speech, you do not need to keep the three elements in this strict chronological order. You can rearrange them any one of six different ways to suit where you want to put the emphasis.

The Goldilocks principle

As you tell the story, you will find that the Goldilocks Principle is a useful instant structure to your speech or presentation.

You can break each of your sections into three sub-sections – and even go one step further by subdividing those into three different subject areas.

How you choose to do this will depend on how much time you have and also where you want to put the emphasis in what you have to say.

If you don't like the idea of using the structure of a fairy-tale as the basis of a serious presentation, think of it as the **Sudoku Structure**.

The Beethoven Imperative

Sometimes, this Goldilocks Principle can be emphasized with the Beethoven Imperative – dee-dee-dee-dum! – by adding a punchline after the three points to summarize, emphasize or draw a conclusion.

Braindumping and research

Every good presentation or speech is based on extensive research and braindumping.

The quality of what you incorporate into what you finally decide to say is relative to the quality and quantity of what you choose to leave out.

The name of the game

Respect your audience. They have given you the privilege of the platform and you must honour that.

Familiarize yourself with aspects of their culture, be aware of their sensitivities, and take the time to reflect on what you want to say from the perspective of the people you are addressing.

Once upon a time ...

Now that you have the outline of your story and have identified the key messages, what can you do to hold their attention?

This is the skill of the story-teller, and the subject of the next chapter.

6

Tell me a story

Are you sitting comfortably? Then I'll begin

For an older generation of British children and listeners to the BBC around the world, these were the opening words of 'Listen with Mother', a children's radio programme that was broadcast every weekday afternoon from 1950 to 1982.

Over a period of time, the words became synonymous with attracting the attention of a group before starting to address them – emphasizing the point that you will learn later about using stagecraft to settle the audience and win their focus and attention.

In most societies around the world, story-telling is still an important part of bringing up children because children love stories, and because much of their learning – especially of culture, tradition, morals and behaviour – comes from stories.

As adults, we continue to learn from stories whether these are set out in books or acted out in plays and films. It's those opening moments of a story that capture the imagination:

Once upon a time ...

Many years ago, in a far and distant land ...

One bright morning, I woke up and looked around me to find that ...

The opening sentences of your speech or presentation will determine whether you can truly engage with your audience.

While teachers and trainers estimate that they can hold the attention span of an adult class for 45 minutes; television producers reckon that they have three minutes to draw you in to a drama programme; multi-media designers calculate that the average time people take to absorb web-page content is between three and five *seconds*.

So, how long do you have, as a speaker, to capture the attention of your audience?

This will depend on many factors, such as the ages of the people, the size of the group and the nature of the occasion. But, even allowing for the variations that these factors present, your objective doesn't change: get their attention, and hold on to it.

There are at least ten ways to seize the attention of the audience.

Tork and Grunt were considering how Grunt should open his speech at the hustings.

Grunt was convinced that one of the social problems with the tribe arose from the fact that the women were working too hard and taking on too much responsibility.

Not only were they raising the children, preparing food and making warm clothing for the family, they were also the only ones who knew how to catch fish in the lake. This meant they were working very long hours.

Grunt wanted to explore ways of sharing the responsibilities, though he drew the line at the thought of women hunting. For Grunt, that degree of emancipation would be a step too far.

Tork and Grunt were sitting on the ledge in front of Tork's cave while Grunt explained his ideas:

> *'The way I see it, Tork, I should get straight to the point and appeal to the women as mothers. I thought I'd say something like:* "*I want to talk to you today about organizing the day-to-day work of the tribe. I want to give our wives and daughters more*

time to be mothers and ease the burden and pressures of the everyday life." How d'you think that sounds, Tork?'

Tork wondered whether Grunt was finally starting to understand. He congratulated his old comrade:

*'That's what is called the **Direct Approach**, going straight to the point and getting the audience's attention immediately.*

*'Another way of doing it is what's called the **Indirect Approach**. That's when you start by talking about something that's completely away from the subject and then come back to the main point. What you could say is:*

"I want new clothes. I love to look good. When I'm wearing a smart cloak I know I look good and I feel good. But look at me today! This cloak is falling apart. I need new clothes!

Tork shows Grunt a different way to start his speech

"So, I went into the store of hides and skins and picked out three fine, well-tanned pelts that will make a beautiful warm cloak for the winter. But there's a problem.

"Designing clothes and sewing them is difficult and delicate work that's always been done by the women of the tribe, ever since Chat and Wizpa brought those skills to us when their tribe joined us here. It's not something that we men have ever mastered.

"But our women don't have enough time for such tasks. So, we need to re-think the whole way we organize our village work so that we men take on some new responsibilities and let the women have time for the work that they enjoy."'

Grunt's face lit up.

'That's great, Tork! I can imagine people sitting there wondering what on earth I'm going to talk about standing there wrapped in that tatty old cloak. It really gets people listening, doesn't it?

'But listen, Tork, suppose I started by saying something like: "What do I have to do to get myself a new cloak?" I'd really get their attention with that, wouldn't I?'

'Definitely, Grunt. And using a provocative question can be a third way of opening a speech. You already have people thinking about the question and wondering what you are going to propose as the answer. If you start the way you suggested just now, you'd be combining two classic openings: the Indirect Opening and the Question Opening.'

'So, tell me, Tork, are there any other ways you can start a speech and get the audience going? Or is it just those three?'

Tork took a handful of pebbles and counted out ten on the ground. Then he picked up seven, leaving three in the dust.

'That's the first three, Grunt, and there are seven more. Let me tell you a story about what I once did.'

Grunt looked intrigued.

'Go on then, I'm interested.'

'Let me tell you a story about what I once did'

Tork grinned as he put the fourth pebble on the ground. Grunt was puzzled.

'So, come on then Tork, what's number four? I'm dying to know.'

'I just used it, Grunt, didn't you hear me? I said: "Let me tell you a story about what I once did." That's the fourth way of starting a speech: tell them a story, especially one about yourself.'

'Oh yes, I see. You're right, you really got me interested. So, what's number five?'

Tork took two pebbles and laid them down side by side very deliberately.

'The next two are opposites. There's putting your presentation into an historical context; and the other is looking into the future and getting people to use their imagination.'

73

Grunt pondered this for a moment while he thought of how he might use these techniques.

'Suppose I started off by saying something like: "A few years ago, our way of life was dramatically changed by the gifts that Wizpa and Chat brought us when they taught our women the new skill of fishing."'

Tork nodded enthusiastically:

'Perfect, Grunt. You've put the situation into an historical context that people can either remember having heard themselves, or else they've heard people talking about it.

'What about looking into the future?'

'Well, how about if I sort of looked at them all, quite intently, and then said: "One day, we'll keep animals in field with hedges round, so we don't have to chase all over the hillside hunting.

'"One day, we'll plant fruits and vegetables near to home, so we don't need expeditions to go looking for them in the wild.

'"And maybe, one day, we'll even put fences in the lake, so the fish can't swim away, and we'll never worry about finding enough food again. That's all in the future.

'"Today I'm going to talk to you about my plans for making our lives easier right now."

'I must say, Tork, that sounded very powerful. I'm starting to enjoy this now!'

Tork looked straight back at Grunt and said:

'They say that if you give a man a fish, you feed him for a day, but if you teach him to fish, you feed him for life.'

'Exactly my point, Tork. The more people who know how to fish ... hang on! You're doing it again, aren't you? That's another way of starting a speech, isn't it?

'*You can use a well-known saying as an opening, can't you? You almost caught me out again. But you know me: once bitten – twice shy. There, that's another old proverb! You won't catch me out again, Tork.*'

At last, Tork felt he was getting through to Grunt. He said:

'*When you're looking at two options, such as the way things were once and the way they are today, or if you're talking about two options in the future, you can compare them and contrast them. You talk about the benefits or drawbacks of one against the other. That can work well.*'

Grunt's face lit up as he grabbed the last two pebbles from out of Tork's hand and slapped them down on the ground to complete the pattern:

'*I'm enjoying this now, Tork. I can see how getting the right opening helps in two ways: it helps the audience to relax, and it helps the speaker to feel confident. There! Did you hear that – that was Compare and Contrast in action, wasn't it?*

'*You know what Alto said on the day he nominated me: "We must learn from the past and live in the future." That's become a real motto for the tribe, y'know.*

'*And now I've got the last ones, haven't I? Using a saying or proverb, number nine; and using a famous quotation, that's number ten?*

'*I used those famous words that Alto said about the past and the future. I could use a famous quotation like that to start off. Imagine! If I use the words of a famous person then people will think of me just in the same way as they thought of him, won't they?*'

Grunt was well away now, chattering enthusiastically. Tork replied in a more sober tone:

'*That's part of the idea, Grunt – but not exactly the same way. Alto was a great leader.*'

'Maybe, but he couldn't even hunt a mouse or a platypus.'

'That's not generally part of the leader's job, Grunt.'

'No, I suppose not, come to think of it. But you know what, Tork? You spreading those pebbles on the floor has got me thinking …

'It's easy to think in tens because you can count tens off on your fingers, can't you? Do you think people will always reckon in tens, even when there are tens of tens, and tens of tens of tens, like the huge herds of wildebeest on the plains?'

'I'll tell you what I think, Grunt: I think that one day they'll have words for tens of tens that will make it easier to think in large groups—'

'Oh, Tork, that sounds very complicated. Leave that to the young-sters to work out. Ten's about all I can cope with, so let's go

Grunt practises the perfect way to start his speech

through all the ten options we've just been through, and then I'll work out which ones I can use.'

And with that, Tork sat back and watched Grunt trying out new ideas and approaches with a new-found enthusiasm.

Conversation, not commentary

Capturing the immediate attention of your audience is vital. Once you've achieved that, there's then the matter of holding on to it.

Remember that you are telling a story. Remember the Goldilocks Principle. Then you'll find that the rhythm of the triads carries the audience along in anticipation.

They try to guess what's coming next – and this in itself holds their attention.

Remember to keep to a story-telling mode and you'll understand why the strap-line I use for my own company, Messages into Words, is *'Telling the corporate story'*.

You'll find that holding the audience comes more easily if you make a point of remembering the WIIFY (what's in it for you?) factor you learned in Chapter Three. The audience are sitting there, asking themselves what's in it for them – and if you keep reminding them of the relevance to their situation, then you pull them back and hold their attention. Some of the phrases that work well include:

This is important to you because ...

What does this mean in your department?

You may wonder why I'm going on about this – let me tell you ...

Here's something that will help you ...

I'll tell you something many people find really useful ...

Have you ever considered what would happen if ...?

How will this affect you?

The reason that questions work well is because every good speech is a conversation.

Even though the audience are not interacting vocally with you, they have a conversation going on in their heads, questioning things that you say and responding to questions that you put into their minds.

You will have seen presentations where the presenter has *not* been a story-teller holding a conversation with his audience, but instead has been a commentator on the sequence of slides that he puts on the screen.

This is not the way to deliver an effective presentation, and yet it's what many presenters do. They want the slides to tell the story, and they reduce their presentation to commentary.

You'll learn more about that in the second section of this book, when you consider how a presentation or speech should be illustrated.

But before you move on to the next chapter, just remember one key point about this: it is *you* who are telling the story; the slides are there to add illustration to your story. *You* establish the interaction and make the conversation; the slides are a visual commentary.

It should NEVER be the other way around.

Sadly it usually is the other way around! In every country and in every language, you will see presenters screen their slides and read their words. Can *you* help me to change that?

I am leading a campaign to inoculate the world against that epidemic, which is often referred to as Death by PowerPoint. But enough of this for the moment; I can feel myself getting passionate about it and there's time to talk about the effective use of PowerPoint in the next section. For now, let's come back to the point about conversation.

Connect with your audience with the words that you use. Have a conversation. Ask the questions and then give them the answers. This is how you involve them in the story.

Make them part of the solution to the challenges that you are describing, as you take them on a journey from where they have been in the past to where you see them, with you, in the future. This is what speech-writing and presentation-drafting are all about.

It's not about communicating information – there's a photocopier, email and the internet to do that.

It's about the action that is needed to create change, and it's about the amazing story of the journey you make together.

And they all lived happily ever after

That's the way stories end, whether it's a play from Aristotle, a movie from Hollywood, a fairy tale about Goldilocks or a symphony from Beethoven.

And what about your presentation? If you've started well, established a clear structure and led them through the story of the journey from where they were to where you want them to be, what else should you do? How should you draw to a conclusion?

The answer is that you should remind them of the initial context, what you propose should be different in the future, and the process necessary to make that transition.

You don't add anything new, you avoid repeatedly going over old ground, you draw together the logic of the journey, and you emphasize the key points that you have made along the way.

Above all, you make a point of repeating the key messages that you want them to remember.

When Martin Luther King made his famous speech in 1963, he used the classic three-part structure. He set the historical context; he outlined his vision with the phrase '*I have a dream*', using the word *dream* no less than eleven times; and then he made the call for action, repeating the phrase *let freedom ring* twelve times.

His speech said:

This is the way things are.

This is the way they could and should be.

This is what we must do.

Don't end your speech by bemoaning the sad state of things as they have been, and don't make your last words talk about your vision of the way you want things to be. Focus at the end on what needs to be done, on the difference in what people must do and the difference in the way they must think.

Remember, that's the objective of any speech: urging people to think differently and act differently.

Moving on

In the past five chapters you've looked at assembling the content and creating the structure for your story. In the next section, you will consider how to illustrate it, and then in the final section, how to deliver it.

Don't panic! Whether you're an elder brother or a mother, a dad or a great-aunt, you've never had a problem with story-telling to the next generation, have you? That's really all there is to it.

And now you've worked out the storyline, you can think about the pictures. But first, take a moment to consider one of the most famous speeches of all time: the Gettysburg Address.

The Gettysburg Address

There are many famous speeches that were made at historic moments through the ages. But few match Abraham Lincoln's Gettysburg address as an example of a presentation designed to change the mindset of a nation.

It is approximately 269 words in length, depending on which of the five drafts you study, and it was delivered in just under two minutes.

Politicians of today's world would do well to note this as a lesson in brevity and conciseness.

As you read through it, you will see examples of triads, alliteration, simile and metaphor creating vivid imagery for his audience.

Below is the simple text; following that you will see an analysis of various figures of speech and literary techniques that Lincoln employed to create this outstanding example of the wordsmith's craft.

Fourscore and seven years ago our fathers brought forth on this continent a new nation, conceived in liberty and dedicated to the proposition that all men are created equal.

Now we are engaged in a great civil war, testing whether that nation or any nation so conceived and so dedicated can long endure. We are met on a great battlefield of that war. We have come to dedicate a portion of that field as a final resting-place for those who here gave their lives that that nation might live. It is altogether fitting and proper that we should do this.

But in a larger sense, we cannot dedicate, we cannot consecrate, we cannot hallow this ground. The brave men, living and dead who struggled here have consecrated it far above our poor power to add or detract. The world will little note nor long remember what we say here, but it can never forget what they did here. It is for us the living rather to be dedicated here to the unfinished work which they who fought here have thus far so nobly advanced. It is rather for us to be here dedicated to the great task remaining before us – that from these honored dead we take increased devotion to that cause for which they gave the last full measure of devotion – that we here highly resolve that these dead shall not have died in vain, that this nation under God shall have a new birth of freedom, and that government of the people, by the people, for the people shall not perish from the earth.

In breaking the text down into a table, we have added some typographical formatting changes to emphasize points and clarify the style so that it is more obvious to analyse.

➤ Four score and seven years ago, our fathers brought forth upon this continent a new nation: conceived in liberty, and dedicated to the proposition that all men are created equal	➤ This is setting the scene with a precise statement of the historical context ➤ The use of the biblical style four score and seven, echoing 'three score years and ten' in Psalm 90, sets a momentous tone ➤ Then the words conceived and created are used, reversing the usage so that the nation is conceived whereas all men are created. Logically, nations are created and men are conceived
➤ Now we are engaged in a great civil war ... testing whether that nation, or any nation so conceived and so dedicated ... can long endure	➤ He reiterates the word conceived to link back to the previous sentence, emphasizing the unique origins of the nation
➤ We are met on a great battlefield of that war	➤ Bringing the audience back to the here and now
➤ We have come to dedicate a portion of that field as a final resting place for those who here gave their lives that that nation might live. It is altogether fitting and proper that we should do this	➤ Establishing the reason for the occasion and the rationale behind it

➤ But, in a larger sense,
  ➤ we cannot dedicate ...
  ➤ we cannot consecrate ...
  ➤ we cannot hallow this ground
	➤ He challenges their right to do this by questioning their right to honour so great a sacrifice. He uses the Rule of Three for emphasis and uses semi-religious words in each line: dedicate, consecrate, and hallow

➤ The brave men, living and dead, who struggled here have consecrated it, far above our poor power to add or detract	➤ He again echoes the powerful word consecrate with its religious connotations, and positions those present as being humbled, by using the phrase 'far above our poor power'
➤ The world will ... ➤ little note, nor long remember, what we say here, ➤ but it can never forget what they did here	➤ He uses the contrasting verbs: ➤ Remember–Forget, Say–Do ➤ As a further twist, he also contrasts tenses: ➤ Present tense – remember what we say ➤ Past tense – forget what they did

➤ It is for us the living, rather, to be dedicated here to the unfinished work which they who fought here have thus far so nobly advanced	➤ Now he contrasts the people who are being honoured with the role of the living; using the word dedicated to refer to the living. This is again a semi-religious word and echoes the concept of consecration in respect of the dead
➤ It is rather for us to be here dedicated to the great task remaining before us	➤ He reiterates the concept of the living being dedicated (to the remaining task)
➤ 1. that from these honoured dead we take increased devotion to that cause for which they gave the last full measure of devotion ➤ 2. that we here highly resolve that these dead shall not have died in vain ➤ 3. that this nation, under God, shall have a new birth of freedom	➤ He uses the Rule of Three to emphasize the tasks ahead for the living: ➤ In (1) he contrasts the devotion of the dead and the devotion of the living ➤ In (2) he emphasizes his idea by talking about the dead not having died in vain ➤ By contrast, (3) avoids any linguistic tricks and makes a simple blunt statement but uses powerful and glorious words
➤ … and that government ➤ of the people ➤ by the people ➤ for the people ➤ shall not perish from the earth	➤ And again, the Rule of Three hammers home the fundamental principle underlying the foundation of the nation Returning to biblical phraseology with the closing words: 'shall not perish from the earth'

Summary

Sagas, epics, fairy tales and legends

There are many kinds of stories. But as Aristotle's Rule of Three taught you, they all have a beginning, a middle and an end. In a presentation, these three sections generally refer to the situation or context, the action and the result.

They can be past, present and future – but you don't have to stick to the chronology of the story. You can tell it in any order you like, often increasing the impact by doing so.

There are many ways to open a presentation. Here are ten ways of ensuring that you capture the audience right from your first words:

1. Direct opening: get straight to the point.
2. Indirect opening: intrigue the audience by starting somewhere else.
3. Dramatic grab: make a challenging statement.
4. Asking a question: get the audience thinking.
5. Story-telling: recount an example, especially from personal experience.
6. Historical: use an actual occurrence from the past.
7. Futuristic: describe how things might be in the future.
8. Saying or Proverb: use a familiar saying to add traditional wisdom.
9. Comparison: compare and contrast two alternative outcomes.
10. Quotation: use a famous quotation to position yourself and add credibility to what you are about to say.

Having grabbed the audience's attention, hold on to it by constantly reminding them of what's in it for them with phrases such as:

This is important to you because …

Here's something that will help you …

Have you ever considered what would happen if …?

When you come to the end of your speech or presentation, remind people about your purpose and reiterate what you want them to do next.

PART TWO

From chalkboard to embedded video

Introduction

In the words of Edward Tufte: '*Power corrupts, PowerPoint corrupts absolutely*!' Tufte is a professor emeritus of statistics, graphic design, and political economy at Yale University, and has been described by the *New York Times* as 'the Leonardo da Vinci of Data'. Although his work on cognitive style is revolutionary, it still languishes for want of uptake from the thousands of people around the world who regularly make presentations or deliver speeches.

But while the speakers hesitate, audiences who have suffered the torture of ill-conceived PowerPoint presentations are restless, and the revolutionaries like myself are whipping up dissent.

PowerPoint is a wonderful tool for manipulating visual imagery – but it is frequently abused.

In this section you will learn about the principles of communication and how visual support can work for your audience. You will also learn how it can work against you and get in the way of your message.

You've learned how to tell your story; now let's add some pictures.

7

'Speaker support'

How to present content

Teaching and presenting are very similar. In both cases the objective is to change the mindset of the audience.

In the presentation scenario, you are probably limited to two options when choosing how to deliver the content that you want to communicate. One is mainly aural, the other mainly visual.

These are recognized as two of the ways that people learn: learning by hearing and learning by seeing. (The third method of learning is *kinaesthetic* – learning by doing.)

However, when the brain tries to assimilate two teaching methods at the same time, there are complications. And in a typical presentation scenario, the audience is expected to absorb the spoken word in conjunction with words on the screen.

Does this work?

First, consider what happens when *aural* and *kinaesthetic* learning are combined.

Robert and Rosemary were off for a romantic weekend when a knocking sound started somewhere at the back of the car. Rosemary turned to Robert with a worried look on her face:

'Darling, what's that knocking sound?'

'I don't know but I'm sure it's nothing to worry about.'

However, the noise grew louder and the steering wheel started to shudder. Rosemary let out a worried shriek:

'Oh, my goodness! Pull over, Robert! This is awful!'

Robert steered the car to the roadside and they both leaped out and ran to the back of the car. Rosemary was alarmed to see that car was leaning over because the rear nearside tyre was completely flat.

'It's a puncture; I'll call the roadside assistance,' she said.

Robert's male pride swelled up.

'Nonsense, it's only a puncture and I can change a wheel. Just need to find where the jack is stowed in this car. It'll be in the back somewhere, underneath our suitcases, I expect.'

And while Robert lined the luggage up by the roadside and carefully laid Rosemary's little black dress on the back seat of the car, she took the car manual out from the glove compartment and began to read up the section entitled 'How to Change a Wheel'.

Robert found the jack and was trying to work out how it fitted together, while Rosemary was reading him the instructions from the manual:

'First ensure that the handbrake is ON and that the car is in first gear. Insert the crank A into the d-section on the cantilever B. Robert, are you listening?'

'I think I've worked it out, just give me a minute. I think it works this way.'

Robert replied as he fiddled with the screw section that operated the lifting mechanism. Rosemary became more agitated:

'Are you sure that's the right bit? It says you have to put A into B and I can't see that's what you're doing. Why don't you listen a moment instead of just trying to work it out?'

> *'Look, Rosemary, just be quiet a moment. I know what I'm doing; I can see how this works. Look: if this bit goes in here and turns round, then this other bit expands to lift the car up.'*

> *'Just listen a moment will you? Let me tell you how you're supposed to do it ...'*

The argument continued while Robert tried to work it out kinaesthetically and Rosemary tried to give him information in words. Rosemary couldn't see that Robert needed to switch off the aural messages that she was giving him so that he could concentrate on hands-on learning. At the same time, Robert didn't realize that he might do well to pause in his patently futile fumbling and listen for a moment to his wife's clear instructions.

I'm sure you can think of instances where you've been trying to absorb a message through one of the senses, while someone has been trying to give you the same message through another of the senses. Your brain can't handle it all because it is concentrating almost exclusively in the particular way that you have told it to learn.

Now imagine yourself listening attentively to a presentation, when suddenly data appears on the screen. Immediately, your reception switches from aural to visual. If you had been handed a sheet of data while the presenter was in the middle of talking, you'd probably have said something like:

> *'Hang on a minute; I need a moment to study this and take it all in.'*

But that isn't the way it works when you are watching a typical business presentation.

Academic research on learning capability

In 2003, Edward Tufte wrote a revolutionary essay entitled 'The Cognitive Style of PowerPoint' (Graphics Press). His theory built on the earlier work of Professor John Sweller at the University of New South Wales in Australia.

Sweller formulated and developed the Cognitive Load Theory, which deals with the ability of the human brain to assimilate information. This theory has been developed by his department with continuing research, which shows that the human brain processes and retains more information if it is digested in **either** its verbal **or** its written form, but **not** through both at the same time.

This is sombre reading for anyone who has depended on PowerPoint as the basic structure of a presentation.

Furthermore, the idea of using visual information goes back many years. Teachers have always sought to find ways to disseminate the data, examples and visual material that form an essential part of their teaching content.

Going back to 'chalk and talk'

One of the first presentations you heard as a child possibly came from teaching that was delivered in the form of a sermon in a church, or preaching in a mosque, synagogue or temple.

Preachers and philosophers traditionally communicated their ideas verbally, sometimes using metaphors and visual images to make their point.

Jesus used examples drawn from life around him of fisherman, farmers and – famously – wild flowers, when he said: '*Consider the lilies of the field, how they grow: they neither toil nor spin; and yet I say to you that even Solomon in all his glory was not arrayed like one of these.*'

Here is a simple metaphor that lives on, even after 2,000 years.

In ancient times, communication relied heavily on metaphor to create its imagery. Aristotle, Plato, Virgil and Seneca all used the metaphor of a community of honey bees as a model of human society.

In modern society, you will find that traditional societies use metaphor constantly in the practice of saga and story-telling that remain an essential way in which these cultures are sustained.

But how can you share images like this *visually*, unless you are either out in the open air where you can point to the examples all around you, or else use vivid *verbal* descriptions?

Verbal description might work if you are, like Aristotle, talking about a swarm of bees. It doesn't work well if you are considering a graph, a spreadsheet or a battle formation.

Yet despite this, it was centuries before easy ways were found to share detailed information with an entire group at the same time. It would appear that the first appearance of a blackboard and chalk was in American military academies in the early nineteenth century, where these were used to describe military campaigns.

The earliest use of a blackboard in the classroom is generally attributed to James Pillans, headmaster and geography teacher at the Royal High School of Edinburgh later that century. In his geography textbook, published in 1854, he describes how he illustrated his lessons with the use of a blackboard and coloured chalks.

For the following hundred years, teachers and lecturers relied on the blackboard to record and display key messages, diagrams and data relevant to their subject. The phrase '*chalk and talk*' is still commonly used to describe a teaching style of minimal interactivity, in which the presenter simply writes on the board and talks about the information.

It's a reasonably effective way to share data – but it's not very stimulating. To the present day, this style has persisted as a formal teaching method in many schools, colleges and universities around the world, sometimes with boards or flip charts, and sometimes with projectors.

It was the arrival of the overhead projector (OHP) that revolutionized the presentation of visual content.

Information could be transferred on to 'transparencies' and projected on to a screen, so that the audience could follow the teaching more easily.

By glancing down to the OHP plate before them, speakers could see exactly what was appearing on the screen and could easily cover-up or disclose sections of the page. They could point out a detail on a transparency, and their directions were immediately visible to the audience, on the screen.

The added bonus was that speakers could continue facing their audience without having to turn their back on the group.

However, while the chalk-written handwriting was by and large visible to the entire class without difficulty, presenters often yielded to the temptation to load an increasing volume of information onto their transparencies, so that sections of the presentation could become an illegible data dump. The classroom cry of *'Can you all see this at the back?'* was replaced by the ominous phrase: *'This may be a bit small for some of you, so let me read it out!'*

Thus was born the first challenge for the modern presenter: the temptation to read the screen.

And the next development only served to increase this temptation when, in the middle of the last century, the overhead projector was superseded by the arrival of the 35mm photographic slide.

The semi-automated Kodak Carousel projector made it possible for slides to be advanced and controlled remotely with the click of a remote button at the end of a control flex. This was a revolutionary innovation. From sales pitches to military briefings, presentations moved into a new technological era.

But the advance had its drawbacks.

You needed the support of a studio to produce your slides; no longer was there the option to hand-write key points straight onto the OHP transparencies with a felt-tipped pen. This made the process of producing a presentation more complex.

Furthermore, presenters were continually peering over their shoulder or turning their back on the audience so that they could see what was on the screen. It was the same problem as had existed in the classroom with the blackboard: each time teachers turned to write on the board, they jeopardized the essential human connection of facing their audience and interacting with them, and ran the risk that people in the back row would start talking among themselves.

Mechanical process made it simple to reproduce spreadsheets containing any amount of data. This meant that, like its OHP predecessor, the 35mm slide was frequently used as a data-dump. Presenters put all their energy into their visuals, and little thought into the story they wanted to tell.

They forgot, or at least overlooked, the *underlying purpose* of their presentation. Presentations became a sequence of visuals explained by commentary, rather than a conversation illuminated by visuals.

Some of these problems might have been solved when Microsoft first developed and launched PowerPoint. At least it had now become possible for presenters to glance down at the laptop screen in front of them and let the data projector automatically put the slides on the screen. This way, presenters could continue to face the audience, just as they would have done with an OHP.

Sadly, all the old habits die hard.

Today, many presenters still use their slides as data dumps, overloading them with too much information. Then they turn their backs on the audience to read the screen, as if they were Elementary School teachers helping young children learn new words.

The Medium is the Message

This was the intended title of Marshall McLuhan's seminal work of the 1960s, heralding the birth of a revolution in communications.

According to his son, it was a source of amusement to him that the book came back from the printers with the title misspelt as *The Medium is the Massage*. Rather than correct the error, the author decided that the mistake was supportive of the point he was trying to make in the book – and decided to leave it alone.

The Wikipedia entry for the book condenses its message succinctly:

Its message, broadly speaking, is that historical changes in communications and craft media change human consciousness.

This may still sound extreme, but I have no hesitation in suggesting that PowerPoint has changed how people communicate in Western society.

Increasingly, people talk, write and maybe even think in bullet points. The skill of eloquence, the natural flow of verbal argument, and the process of simple logic have all been eroded because of a lack of structure in conversation and debate.

Two options for delivering your message

At the beginning of this section, you learned that the two learning methods normally associated with presentations are *aural* and *visual*. When you are planning a presentation, you have to decide how you are going to tell your story – whether it will be the screen or the voice that will communicate the essential facts of your message.

Should you choose to create a presentation that depends largely on the *visual* medium, then you need to realize that you are talking about a big budget production. *Visual messaging* is the domain of the film and television documentary, utilizing *oral* content to expand on and explain the *visual* imagery. This demands a wide skill-set, from scriptwriting and voice-over, to photographic and editing ability.

On the other hand, if your *voice* is going to tell the story, and you plan to add *visual* material to illustrate key points, then you must ensure that you respect all the research on Cognitive Load and do not allow a conflict between what you want to say and what you put on the screen.

You've probably already decided – or had it dictated by company policy – that you'll deliver a PowerPoint presentation.

There's nothing new about adding pictures to illustrate a lecture. Back in the Victorian era, Stanley talked to excited audiences about his search for Livingstone in Central Africa, and illustrated his lecture with hand-painted lantern-slides.

But, apart from the issue of corporate policy, *why are you using PowerPoint?*

Back to basics

You could go to the other extreme and simply give a speech, as did Gandhi, Martin Luther King, Winston Churchill, John F. Kennedy. No slides, no flip charts, not even a chalk-board.

Yet, they moved their audiences from A to B, they changed the mindset of their audiences, and they made them think and act differently. Perhaps you're not entirely happy to do that. You're looking for help, for what is neatly termed 'Speaker Support' – something to help the presentation flow, to give your talk a logical structure, and to give visual clarification to various points.

At the same time, you'd like to be able to give the audience notes as a handout at the end, so that they can refer back to your presentation in the future.

This all sounds smart enough ... except that you are describing a number of functions; and, despite the way most people use it, no single medium can cover all these areas:

> *You want a structure, set out in a way that you can follow easily.*

> *You want a reminder of the points you want to make.*

> *You want data set out to support your argument.*

> *You want examples on which you can comment.*

> *You want visual imagery to enhance your script.*

> *You want useful material for the audience to take away with them afterwards.*

Some of this could be described as Speaker Support, some as Audience Support and some as Presentation Support. No single medium can fulfil all three roles – yet that is what people expect of PowerPoint.

If you want to kill the audience, use bullets

Every week, tens of thousands of presentations are made, based on the PowerPoint process of bullet points, clip-art and corporate graphics.

Most of these are based on communicating data, rather than communicating knowledge and ideas. While the computing industry has made the step-change from talking about *data-processing* to talking about *knowledge-management*, the authors of most presentations have yet to learn the difference.

Every week, thousands of audiences suffer Death by PowerPoint: they are *Killed by Bullets*.

If you want the visual content to tell the story, you're looking at a seriously substantial multi-media budget. You can do it yourself, as long as you are confident that you can be a director, a visualizer, a multi-media technician, a scriptwriter and a voice-over artiste.

You may need to be pretty nifty with a camcorder and a digital camera as well.

Otherwise, go back to basics and start by drafting your storyline.

Arrows, not bullets

Audiences don't want to be splattered with the buckshot of random data; they want the speaker to lead them with clear and definite arrows from A to B.

You will not create a powerful presentation by starting with a deck of slides. You'll do it by first deciding what you want people to do or think at the end of your presentation, and then telling your story to move them from where they are now to where they need to be to reach your objectives.

With most PowerPoint presentations, there's a tendency for the speaker to support what's on the screen. It should be the other way around, with the screen supporting the speaker.

So, what is speaker support?

Whether it's a blackboard, a flip chart, or a projector and screen, what is frequently called *speaker support* should actually be called *audience support*.

Speaker support is a misnomer, which is why the words are in quotes at the top of this chapter. You will learn about *real* speaker support later, when you look at various elements of performance and delivery, and consider what you need at hand to keep you on track.

The reason that half of this book is devoted to talking about how and why you are telling your story is because *your story is more important than its delivery and its illustration*. Let me tell you why I decided on this principle when I was planning this book.

What makes a bad presentation?

When I'm not scripting management conferences or working on a corporate video, I sometimes train groups of managers on *How to deliver Powerful and Effective Presentations*. I start by asking them what makes a bad presentation, and list all the ideas that they come up with. Here are some typical responses:

I sit there wondering why I'm wasting my time.

It's not relevant to me.

The slides are confusing.

They just read what's on the screen and I can do that myself, thank you!

I've heard it all before.

He/she's repeating him/herself.

My groups very rarely mention voice, or body language, or what the professionals call *Platform Skills*, except for the regular complaint about **reading the screen**. The comments are nearly all about the *content* of the presentation, not about the *delivery*.

When they realize this, and look at the list I have jotted on the flip chart as they have been participating with their comments, they are usually surprised, especially if they have already been on other Presentation Skills courses and have been taught stage techniques and breathing exercises.

It's not about presentation.

Gandhi had a light and tremulous voice. Churchill's sonorous tones could well have been soporific to listen to. Dr Stephen Hawkins speaks through a synthesizer. Yet all three have delivered messages that are gripping, spellbinding and world-changing.

In order to change people's mindset and make them think or act differently, you need to put across a convincing argument, logically structured and designed to appeal to the audience.

It's all about content.

It doesn't have to be 'Death by PowerPoint'

A few years ago, the presenter of the BBC's *In Business* programme asked Microsoft spokesperson, Brendan Bush, what audience-testing Microsoft had carried out to evaluate the impact of PowerPoint. His reply was sadly revealing:

> '*It's not something we've paid the most attention to because they're not the ones paying us.*'

This sums up the thinking behind the creation of PowerPoint. It was not designed as a tool to improve the impact and effectiveness of a presentation; it was designed to assist the presenter, because it is the presenters, not the audience that buy and use the PowerPoint programme. Hence, PowerPoint is generally referred to in the events industry as *speaker support* and, sadly, that is the way most people use it.

Don't get me wrong! As a creative person, I love the flexibility and potential of PowerPoint. It's just that, in more than a dozen years in the communications business, I have seen perhaps five or six examples of good use of the medium – and far too many others where the speaker would have done a better job if he had sat down, pressed the Advance button on the laptop and simply let the audience read what was on the screen.

PowerPoint is like a box of paints. Give the box to a portrait artist and he can produce an insightful likeness. Give the same box to a novice and you will probably struggle to recognize the person in the picture.

It doesn't even have to be PowerPoint

Remember that the purpose of your presentation is to change the mindset of your audience.

You will do this by communicating your message with words that can – if you choose – be enhanced with images, props or stories of previous experiences.

I was once involved with the sales conference of a healthcare company at which a new incentive programme was being announced. Promotional schemes like this are often referred to as working like a carrot – rather than a stick – to entice a donkey to get moving.

When the Sales Director announced the scheme, he walked through the room tossing out bags of raw carrot sticks into the audience while he talked about the different rewards that the sales teams could receive for different levels of achievement.

This proved to be a powerful way to make the message memorable at minimal cost.

Tork plans Audience Support for Grunt's party political meeting

Tork and Grunt were sitting on the ledge outside the caves. Grunt's confidence was growing now that he had a clear idea of his strategic messages.

His platform would be Family Values and re-organizing the daily programme of activities so that there would be more time for child-rearing and education, and so that the men and women of the tribe could each make their own, specialist contributions.

Grunt was outlining his ideas to Tork:

> 'What I want to do, Tork, is give them an idea of what it will be like if we can change the way we organize life here on the mountain. I want to them to have a picture of how it will look if the women have time to play with the children and to make the tribe's cloaks and tunics. I'm not sure that everyone will have the same vision as I have, and then they won't be able to imagine it the way I see it.'

Tork smiled:

> 'Grunt, have you noticed the words you're using? Have a **picture** – how it will **look** – have the same **vision** – able to **imagine** it...?
>
> 'All the words you use are about **sight**, and there's a way we can create that vision – to use your word – so that everyone will remember your speech and it becomes part of tribal society.'

Grunt looked sceptical:

> 'I'm not sure I know what you're getting at – d'you mean something like the cave-paintings of us out hunting?'

Tork replied quickly:

> 'Exactly! We'll paint a picture on the rock-face behind where you're going to speak, and we'll make it depict the ideal society that you want to create for everyone. What we're doing is creating the **context**.
>
> 'Stop being "visual" for a moment and think of it geographically. You are one of the original valley people, so to the audience you represent an important part of the tribe's history. They also know where they are at the moment and they know that life's tough. What you are describing is a better life and a better community in the future.'

'So you mean that we should have a cave-painting of what that better life looks like?'

'Exactly. And we'll get all our election team involved in painting it, so that they can feel part of it.'

'But what if it rains? Won't the painting wash off?'

Tork looked at Grunt with an air of sheer despondency:

'It won't rain at this time of year. Honestly, Grunt, I despair of you! Trust me, this will be fun.'

Grunt uses a powerful visual aid to put his message across: 'I think the women should be able to spend more time with the children'

Visual support can be in the form of posters, banners, handouts and even good old-fashioned flip charts.

Props can be anything from something you pull out of your pocket, to the total environment in which you are making your presentation.

It's about adding more to your words. It is an opportunity to use experiences and visual teaching, in addition to auditory teaching.

What follows in the next chapter is an outline of how to create power-ful and complementary *audience support* and *presentation support*.

The discussion of *speaker support* is where it belongs, as part of the third section of the book, where you will learn about the delivery of your presentation.

Summary

It's all about content

When you go to a restaurant and the spread on the buffet looks tempting, you're impressed. If the colours are inviting and the aromas enticing, then you want to help yourself.

However, if the food is tasteless or bland then any thoughts about appearance and aroma are completely forgotten and you spit it out.

Your presentation is, like the buffet meal, made up of both *substance* and *appearance*.

In the last century, chefs in hotels and restaurants worried far too much about how their dishes looked and far too little about how they tasted. Thankfully, times have changed and today restaurants know that their customers have far more discerning palates than they had in the past.

Don't fall into the same error; get the contents and the recipe right, long before you worry about visual presentation.

You don't want your audience metaphorically to spit out and reject what you have to say. You want them to remember all the key points of your message in the same way they can remember the fresh-boiled crab on Fisherman's Wharf in San Francisco, the charcoal spitroasted lamb at a rooftop taverna in the Plaka district of Athens, or the hot bacon rolls from a stall at an early morning antiques market in London.

To make your presentation memorable, add visual triggers. Use simple gimmicks and create a theme – but above all, remember that these should complement and not conflict with your vocal message.

Remember that people can more easily absorb communication if it is coming at them through one medium at a time.

8

How to create 'audience support'

Creating structure

By now you will be fully aware that PowerPoint is not a vehicle for telling your story, unless you add a sound track – which is certainly an option worth exploring in some circumstances.

Unfortunately, it has become commonplace for people to expect to be able to look at a PowerPoint presentation, even if they have been unable to be in the audience when it was being delivered, and still be able to follow, interpret and understand the speaker's message.

In fact, there is no reason why you should expect to be able to understand the speaker's argument by watching a deck of PowerPoint slides that have been produced for the specific purpose of illustrating a spoken presentation. The slides should have been specifically produced for clarification and impact during the talk. Without the spoken word, you should expect them to be about as comprehensible as watching a television drama with the sound turned off.

The reason that people expect to be able to circulate the deck of slides, as an alternative to delivering their presentation personally, is because so many speakers start with slides and then work on the words to support them. WRONG!

As you have learned in the first part of this book, you start with the story. Once you have worked out the story, you decide on the illustrations.

Start with your bullets

Just don't start by putting bullets into PowerPoint, or in the case of Apple, Keynote®.

Working from the braindumping that you started with, jot down the key headings for the various areas of your presentation. Work out what visual material will support these headings and then start to construct a sequence.

You don't need something on the screen the whole time. Watch any video of Steve Jobs, CEO of Apple Computers, and you'll see how he uses visual support for occasional headings, blended with video illustrations and entertainment. Most of the time there is nothing on the screen at all.

And never a bullet in sight.

Steve Jobs is not a brilliant presenter because he was born that way; he's just learned to have a conversation with the audience and not let the visuals get in the way of the message. This leads us to the ten commandments of PowerPoint:

➤ The First Commandment of PowerPoint
  Bullets are *speaker support*, not *audience support*

Starting with PowerPoint

Unfortunately, most executives don't start their business presentation with the story; they start with their deck of slides.

Since many presentations are about a hierarchy, a process or a structure, it is inevitable that this is more easily represented with a diagram than with paragraphs of words. Hence flow charts can be useful. They can encapsulate something diagrammatically in such a way that it is easier to comprehend than if it is set out in text.

Using flow charts

The danger of flow charts is that they can fall victim to wishful thinking.

They can portray the situation as the speaker would like it to be, not as it is. And they can depict future progress and developments as they might evolve in an ideal world, without attention to probability or even possibility.

There is a school of thought in the USA that the escalation and intensification of the Iraq war are the result of over-simplified Pentagon briefings that were based on PowerPoint.

The following chart, re-drawn for clarity from one that has been widely circulated on the Internet, is allegedly taken from the Pentagon briefing on the war.

In order to capture the whole process from invasion to democracy on one slide, the processes have been reduced to headings. Perhaps there were other slides that went into this in more detail – maybe there was an extensive document that accompanied the slide – but as it stands, It communicates only confusion and wishful thinking.

It reinforces the argument put forward by Garr Reynolds (www.GarrReynolds.com) that there is no reason to expect a deck of slides to be intelligible unless it is accompanied by the presentation script.

Garr is currently an associate professor at a Japanese university teaching Global Marketing and Multimedia Presentation Design. He is one of the trailblazers in the design and execution of presentations, having previously been Manager of Worldwide User Group Relations at Apple Computers.

This diagram clearly demonstrates the danger of flow charts, whether or not it is from a genuine Pentagon briefing. Sadly, given the reliability of the various Internet sources on which it appears, I have no reason to suspect that it is anything other than genuine.

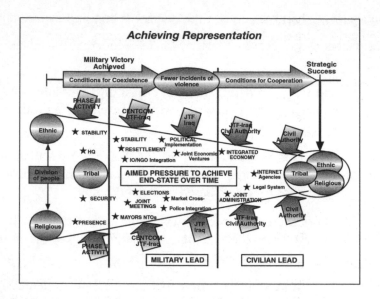

Working from a flow chart

When the presentation is aimed at altering the mindset, to prepare the audience to accept proposed changes, whether these are in processes, channels to market or the way people work together, the story is likely to start with an organization structure or a flow chart.

A flow chart is a conglomeration of a number of simple stages into one overall diagram. Think of it as being similar to an architectural blueprint of a building, or a map of unknown territory.

As we can see in the Pentagon example, the difficulty lies with the fact that there is probably a lot on the chart that needs detailed explanation. If you have lavished hours, days – or even longer – drawing out, re-drafting and detailing the visual, then what you have finally developed could well be a critical document and a plan for the process that you are introducing.

You want people to understand it and use it.

It needs to be detailed. But when you put it up on the screen, there's a problem. If you make the chart easy enough for everyone to see and read, then it is almost certainly over-simplified.

On the other hand, if you add the necessary text and explanations then it goes straight into the category of *'you probably can't read this at the back of the room'*.

When you are faced with a complex plan, diagram or map, you start by wanting to get your bearings and understand the basics of what goes where. Being confronted with the whole picture is a bit like being presented with an encrypted puzzle: you need a moment or two to get your head around it. You want no distractions while you concentrate.

Think back to the earlier example of Robert and Rosemary. He couldn't listen to Rosemary *telling* him how to change the wheel while he was trying to work it out *kinaesthetically*.

Similarly, your audience are not able to listen to you at the same time as they try to figure out a diagram. When it comes up on the screen, the audience needs time to absorb and decode the messages, analysing it step by step. The speaker must stop speaking, pause and give the audience time until the *Ah-hah*! moment when they have grasped the concept, at least in broad terms.

Don't be afraid to give the audience time to study it and come to terms with the various messages embodied in it. Wait until you can see from their faces that they've got the general gist of what the visual is illustrating before you start to talk about it, and explain it yourself.

If the audience is small enough – say, gathered in a compact meeting room – then I would strongly recommend circulating printouts of the visual for every participant so that they can study it closely and easily, without having to strain their eyes to look at the screen.

Another way of working with a flow chart is to build it up on the screen in small stages so that each section can be explained in detail before going on to the next.

KISS – Keep It Simple, Stupid!

Simplicity is everything. Hold on to the architectural analogy, and think of building the picture up starting with the basic outlines and foundations.

107

While you are familiar with your material and with the weeks of work that have gone into developing the complex diagrams, just remember that your audience are not. It's all new to them and they need time. Keep it simple and take it slowly.

This gives us the next two rules of PowerPoint presentations:

➤ The Second Commandment of PowerPoint
KISS – Keep it simple, stupid!
➤ The Third Commandment of PowerPoint
Slow down. Just because you're anxious about being successful, don't rush to get it all over with!

Spreadsheets, graphs, pie charts and diagrams

Most presenters start with a collection of data about which they want to give their personal interpretation.

The reality is that at least 80 per cent of the information on any spreadsheet is probably irrelevant to the presentation, and the only data that the presenter actually needs to display are the specific items on which he or she needs to make a comment.

Years ago, as a young graduate trainee on a training course in North America, I had the privilege of sitting in on the daily management briefing of United Airlines at O'Hare Airport in Chicago. Each morning there was a coast-to-coast link-up to discuss operational data from the previous 24 hours.

This could have occupied many pages of spreadsheets, but it was edited so that the only numbers that appeared on the screen were the ones that differed significantly from the budgeted forecasts. If any of the basic management metrics were on target, then they did not appear on the screen, but if they were notably higher or lower than had been anticipated they would be visible to the whole management team.

It was a simple and highly effective way of sharing data for analysis and comment. Action could be taken to deal with fluctuations, and time did not need to be wasted looking at results and outcomes which were no more or no less than had been expected.

Another way of handling this could be to outline your conclusions before you display any data at all.

Tell the audience what you want to tell them, and then give them the empirical justification for the conclusions that you have reached. This way, when you do put information on the screen, your audience will be thinking about your conclusions rather than trying to work out their own.

Graphs

When you first learned about graphs at school, you learned to interpret them: they either went up, down or stayed the same. The detailed points along the line of a graph are generally not essential to the argument you are making.

Therefore, following the same logic that United Airlines applied to spreadsheets, there is no need to clutter the screen with these details.

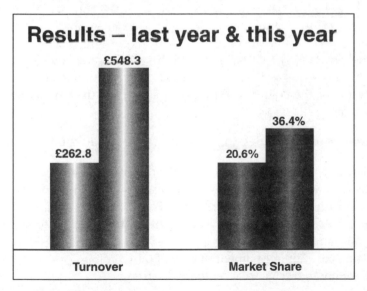

If the essential message is that sales are up on last year by 25 per cent then all the visual needs to show is two cylinders, one of which is 25 per cent taller than the other. Depending on the audience and the corporate policy, it may not even be appropriate to add the actual sales figures – because the *growth* and the *rate of growth* may be more a part of your story than the actual *statistical information*.

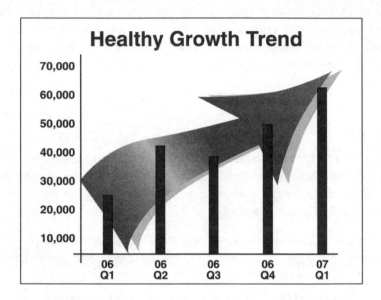

If the message is that sales are rising steadily, and a series of bar charts show this as the average trend, then a bold arrow superimposed over the columns gives a greater impact than the individual chart lines.

This gives us more rules, this time about the visuals themselves:

➤ The Fourth Commandment of PowerPoint
  Decide what you want the visual to say
➤ The Fifth Commandment of PowerPoint
  Put on screen the minimum amount of data needed to illustrate your argument
➤ The Sixth Commandment of PowerPoint
  Simplify the visual to accentuate the trend

Creating impact

Think for a moment about the charity presentation you looked at earlier.

In that scenario, there would be a lot of background information about the plight of the elderly living alone, the numbers involved, ages and demographics, health and needs.

By contrast, the action that is called for is relatively simple: volunteers to give up an occasional evening to visit people in their homes.

In that presentation, a large proportion of the time allotted will be spent getting the audience to understand just what it means to be a lonely person at home alone.

One solution would be to talk about the numbers involved, drawing on government statistics. A conventional PowerPoint presentation on this topic might start with a page of data looking something like this:

Table 61 Services received in the month before interview by whether able to go outdoors and walk down the road

Persons aged 65 and over			*Great Britain: 2001*
Service	Walking outdoors		
	Manages on own	Needs help*	Total
		Percentages	
District nurse/health visitor	3	23	6
Local authority home help	2	16	4
Private home help	9	19	10
Meals-on-wheels	1	6	2
Lunch club	3	5	3
Day centre	2	8	3
Voluntary organisation	1	3	1
Weighted base (000's) = 100%	*7,112*	*1,148*	*8,260*
Unweighted sample	*2782*	*433*	*3215*

* Includes those who cannot go out.
source UK National Statistics "Living in Britain 2001"

There's no denying that there's a powerful message hidden in these numbers – but if the audience is trying to read while at the same time the speaker is talking, the message is diluted. This is a recurring message, as you learned from John Sweller's work on Cognitive Load Theory, described earlier.

This spreadsheet is full of interesting data but in this format it is both difficult to read and makes no real impact. What is more, this is not 'Audience Support' in its true sense because there is no benefit in putting up on screen a mass of statistical information which is difficult to read.

On the other hand, it contains useful data for the speaker to incorporate into his or her delivery, especially by picking out a number of key figures which represent the most important trends. As such, this data should be in the speaker's notes and possibly also incorporated into the material that the audience will take away with them at the end of the presentation, annotated with additional comments and observations.

Here we come to the next rule of PowerPoint, which we already touched on at the end of the last chapter:

➤ The Seventh Commandment of PowerPoint
   Separate *speaker support* from *audience support*

The following slide represents a dramatic improvement on the spreadsheet shown on the previous page:

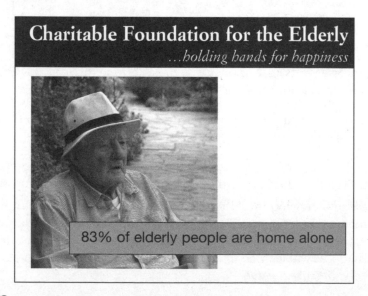

There is no emotional connection in the raw data of a spreadsheet, whereas what this slide delivers is a core message linked to a very emotive picture and just one vital piece of statistical information, extracted and highlighted.

It's a lot better than the previous slide, and can stay on the screen while the speaker goes through various other key figures from the spreadsheet.

But there's still something about this slide that detracts from the impact.

Corporate branding

Most major companies (including Microsoft, in their own guidelines for the layout of PowerPoint slides) recommend that every slide in a set should be on a **template**.

It's something that most presenters do and which, I would suggest, detracts dramatically from the effectiveness of the visual. I know I'm about to go against thousands of corporate policies on corporate branding – but hear me out!

In the example shown above, we have the standard layout that the charity has determined should be the format for every slide in a corporate presentation. This clearly identifies the organization as the **Sponsor** of the occasion, which is important because this is one of the elements that you want people to remember at the end of the presentation.

But it comes at the cost of reducing the impact of each and every slide.

Yes, there's every good reason to give a presentation a strong branding – but that doesn't mean sticking a logo and a strap-line on every single page of a document.

Been there – got the T-shirt

Every slide in this set would – presumably – be branded.

Even though I am a marketing man, and an advocate of strong branding as an essential element in modern corporate life, I would challenge the need to brand every slide in a presentation by surrounding the crucial content within a corporate frame. It's like the logo on clothing or the badge on the car: is it really necessary, or does it diffuse the strength of the message?

I would argue that the use of a standard template:

Reduces the area of the image.

Detracts from the main message by introducing a secondary one – in this case it's 'holding hands for happiness'.

Is boring and repetitive.

When I see a presentation that repeats a corporate strap-line time and time again, I find that I react much the same way as I do seeing slogans on T-shirts – with bored indifference.

You'll see that TV channels are increasingly doing this in the corner of the screen, just to remind you who is responsible for bringing you a programme, and I don't think that it adds anything to the enjoyment of the entertainment. In fact, it can take your eyes and your attention away from the main subject.

Once again, there is an argument for differentiating between what goes on the screen and what goes into a printed handout. But I would suggest that over-branding smacks of egoism rather than the communication of a confident identity.

Good illustrations don't need explanations that hammer home the messages. They convey it all and leave the commentary to the presenter or the audience.

Get the picture?

The next rule of PowerPoint is:

➤ The Eighth Commandment of PowerPoint
Every slide should carry a thousand words

When I first mentioned this rule in a training workshop, one of the group took the statement at face value and asked what size font should be used to get everything on one slide!

In fact, I was of course referring to the saying '*A picture is worth a thousand words*' which was originally coined by an American advertising copywriter in 1927 and cleverly – though fictitiously – attributed to an ancient Chinese proverb.

You can often achieve a far more powerful message if you can make your picture imply the unspoken words. Here is an example of a slide that could support this presentation:

Less is more

This slide is an example of Audience Support, providing a powerful emotional image.

Imagine this coming up on the screen. Imagine how you would immediately identify the problem in your head, and then you would instinctively turn to the speaker to hear the full story that this image encapsulates. This is an illustration to support the story, to inform and entertain the audience by illuminating the reality behind the speaker's message.

115

It is also a slide that forces the audience to focus on the speaker.

Another way to make the emotional connection with the audience is by using video clips. A few years ago this would have been a major technical challenge but now it is a simple matter to incorporate video material. This doesn't have to be a professional piece of edited material. You can make a presentation come to life with a few shots of locations and activities or interviews shot on a camcorder – or even on a mobile phone.

A couple of years ago, I produced a presentation for a global corporate conference using material that the speaker had recorded on his camcorder when he visited the company's main works facility. Even allowing for the cost of studio editing, and the addition of some background music and a professional voice-over, the cost of creating this material for the presentation was a fraction of what it would have cost to use a video production company.

More importantly, the impact of the presentation was immediate, and the message came across as genuine rather than as a piece of slick PR production.

Combining pictures and graphics

When you have a graphic, such as a bar chart, you can humanize the stark geometry – with the result that you dramatically increase the impact of the graphic.

You often see this in television news, which rarely shows basic charts. Instead it takes the information and combines it with appropriate visual imagery to create a picture that tells a clear story. Here are two examples of visually enhanced graphs that have been redrawn based on images in the American newspaper *USA Today*.

In this visual, the bare statistics are made clearer with the use of an illustration in which the chart blocks have been replaced with traffic lanes and cars to show stopping distances.

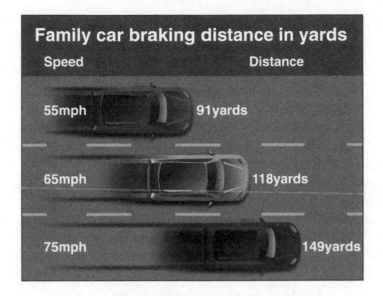

The picture is completely self-explanatory, leaving the speaker free to elaborate on the numbers, give information on the origin and methodology of the information, and continue to expand on the theme of the presentations.

Here is another example, this time about education:

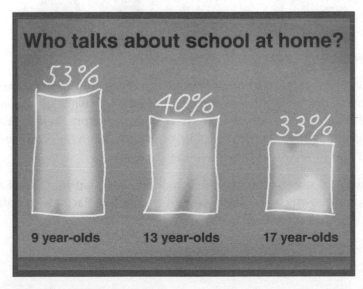

Just three statistics, but the use of the blackboard and chalk immediately puts the numbers into the visual context of the schoolroom. There's no need for the graphic to emphasize the trend because it's obvious: as children get older they are more reluctant to talk about school when they come home.

Using simple icons

In a commercial context, a company can link its visuals to icons that represent its products. This reduces the formality of the presentation while still effectively and accurately communicating the essential information.

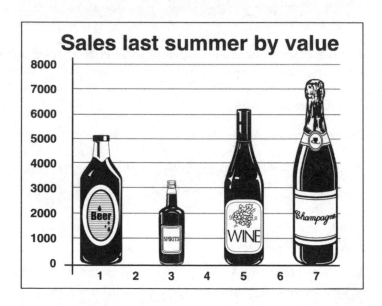

In this example, a drinks company can use simple icons to show its sales so that the eye easily identifies the different categories represented by different areas of the graphic.

➤ The Ninth Commandment of PowerPoint
   Icons simplify and improve the visual presentation of data

Expanding the metaphor

So far, you have looked at ways in which a presentation can create the context for a presentation, and present the data that supports its argument. Another area of Audience Support is in *enhancing the theme* of the presentation.

Many presenters choose a theme to create an intellectual framework, using a metaphor to draw allegorical parallels with their argument. In this context, visual support can be a very effective addition, not only by way of illustration, but also to strengthen the structure of the argument.

Sport is a popular theme for sales conferences, with talk about scoring, teamwork, tactics and winning. Another is 'Struggle in the Face of Adversity'. How many presentations have you seen about facing new challenges, climbing mountains and reaching peaks?

In these examples it is easy to see how visual imagery can set the scene and stimulate the imagination of your audience.

Launching the 'Explorer' range with a strong theme

The team at Red Balloon have been working on ideas for Jacqui's reception and product launch at the Travel Goods Show in Las Vegas. Raj and Malaika have come for a meeting with Jacqui to talk about the theme of the event.

Raj got down to business:

> *'We've given this a lot of thought, Jacqui, and I think you'll like the idea we've come up with. You were with us for the initial braindumping and I think you set us on the right track, so I hope we've not gone off in the wrong direction.*

> *'After you left we carried on, kicking around various ideas. But before we work them into the final version, we'd like to talk about them and explain the rationale behind our thinking. I'll let Malaika run through this; she's been coordinating the project between myself as the writer and the guys in the studio.'*

119

There were just the three of them in the room, so Malaika remained seated to present the team's ideas. She smiled to acknowledge Raj, then looked across the table to Jacqui.

'The formula we've used is the one we generally apply when we're working on a presentation:

'Firstly, we consider the audience: their present situation and what they are looking for.

'Secondly, we look at how you can meet those needs and we develop your core messages by identifying the benefits of your proposition.

'Thirdly, we find a theme that is going to act as a vehicle for your proposition.

'Your audience comprises specialist retailers and department stores, who have seen their market share decline in the face of cut-price competition at the bottom end of the market. They continue to be successful in maintaining their share of the prestige market with your Club Class range – but they know that this market sector is declining and that they need to reach the frequent traveller market you've identified and at which you are directing the Explorer range.

'What we see as the common element in all this is that firstly, the market is changing with new products, greater choice and more channels of distribution.

'Secondly, for the people at your reception, it's all about getting a good share of the market. What we've come up with is a presentation based on the idea that the retailers have been getting a smaller slice of the cake – and that what you are offering them is the opportunity to claim a big slice of this new cake.'

Jacqui nodded cautiously; it sounded as if they'd been giving serious thought to the issues involved. Malaika continued:

'People coming to this reception are expecting the usual thing ... a few drinks, some cocktail nibbles, a presentation about suit-

cases and hand-baggage, and a goody-bag at the end as a souvenir of the occasion.

'We are recommending that you do something totally different, and that's why we've gone for a very different theme for the reception. We're going to invite them to "Tea at the Ritz" by creating the theme of a Palm Court style restaurant.'

Jacqui's face lit up as she grasped the idea of an event that would certainly be out of the ordinary:

'You know, Malaika, Raj, I'm sure we'll attract a lot of press coverage with something as original as that. It sounds so British, and you know what the Americans are like about English traditions.'

'Precisely, Jacqui. But wait ... there's more.'

'I'm all ears!'

Raj clicked the wireless control that was linked to the laptop, and an image came on the screen of bakery shelves laden with cakes and gateaux. He took over from Malaika and continued with the presentation they had prepared.

Customers are spoilt for choice

'*The message, Jacqui, is that the customers are spoilt for choice.*

'*There are ranges of luggage that have been branded with fashion labels, with drink brands and even badged with motoring logos. People can pay pennies for luggage, pick up a free computer bag when they attend a seminar, collect a free overnight bag when they order office supplies, and buy a complete set of suitcases at a knock-down price when they shop for groceries.*

'*It's hurting you and it's hurting your distribution channels. We want to give the trade an image they'll remember, and that's why we came up with tea and cakes. It started when you described how you wanted to use pie charts to show how the distribution has changed. It was only a short step from pie charts to slices of cakes, which led us to this image:*

'*You see, we keep this cake theme and we go from the idea of* choice *to the idea of the* size of the market.'

Jacqui interrupted Raj:

> '*Raj, you don't need to go any further. I want to see this worked up into a full-scale presentation. I want to see the costings – can we really get a five-piece orchestra at an affordable price? – and I want to see invitations all designed on the theme of Tea at the Ritz. I love it! It's different, and it will be the talk of the show. Well done!*'

Raj smiled and added:

> '*Just one more thing, Jacqui. The goody-bags. Can we give them a piece of cake to take away? We want to give them that message: that they're getting their slice of a much bigger cake than they've had before.*'

Jacqui paused for a moment:

> '*There's a cool-bag in the Explorer range. You know, for picnics and things. We've been talking about making a smaller one to take a six-pack – that would be perfect for a slice of cake and all the other literature. Great idea! Brilliant!*'

From this you can see how Red Balloon have used their proposed theme, not only to develop the messages of choice and market share, but also to create an original and memorable theme for the whole event.

> ➤ The Tenth Commandment of PowerPoint
> Use your theme as the visual basis for all your Audience Support and – if appropriate – for the whole event

Summary

Arrows not bullets

Bullet points are the points you want to make in your presentation. They are not information for your audience.

They should form the basis of your speaker notes and should NEVER – repeat NEVER – be up on the screen. They can form headings for the handout materials that you give the audience or send to colleagues after the presentation. But without elaboration they are almost certainly meaningless jottings and should be for your eyes only.

Visual support should be arrows that show the *direction* of your presentation; they lead your audience along the course of your argument, from where they were at the beginning, to the new mindset of the future.

These are the Ten Commandments of PowerPoint:

➤ The First Commandment
  Bullets are *speaker support*, not *audience support*
➤ The Second Commandment
  KISS – Keep it simple, stupid!
➤ The Third Commandment
  Slow down: just because you're anxious about being successful, don't rush to get it all over with!
➤ The Fourth Commandment
  Decide what you want the visual to say
➤ The Fifth Commandment
  Put on screen the minimum amount of data needed to illustrate your argument
➤ The Sixth Commandment
  Simplify the visual to accentuate the trend
➤ The Seventh Commandment
  Separate *speaker support* from *audience support*
➤ The Eighth Commandment
  Every slide should carry a thousand words
➤ The Ninth Commandment
  Icons simplify and improve the visual presentation of data
➤ The Tenth Commandment
  Use your theme as the visual basis for all your audience support and – if appropriate – for the whole event

PART THREE

The flight of the butterflies

Introduction

Many books on presentations begin just here, talking about conquering the nerves and projecting the voice.

This book doesn't, because once you have a clear structure to your presentation, and once you have finalized the visuals to do what they're meant to do, there is not so much left to worry about.

You may still sense those 'butterflies in the stomach' before you take the platform but – with careful preparation and a clear idea of what you want to achieve – those butterflies will flutter away.

It comes back to being structured, being logical and knowing just how you want to connect with your audience.

9

Speeches, messages and preparation

Having a conversation

Grunt's campaign team were gathered around the fire in the moon-light. His wife Natter was watching proudly as her husband outlined the manifesto to the team, who received the new proposals with admiration and enthusiasm.

The outgoing chief, Alto, was the first to comment:

> '*I think this new way of organizing the tribe is an excellent idea, Grunt. You're spot-on when you say that it would be better for everyone if the women spent more time with the children, and there's no reason why we men can't take up fishing. It's just that we've never learned the knack of how to bait the hook and how to know where to cast the line.*'

Grunt smiled broadly and leaned forward with a conspiratorial look on his face:

> '*I reckon that in years to come, men will go off fishing just to escape from the women and the children and all those jobs they have us doing around the cave. We'll be up before dawn and we'll sneak out quietly on our tiptoes, as if we were stalking antelope.*'

Chukka, the cheeky teenager who was already proving his prowess as a hunter and becoming a popular figure with all the girls in the tribe, laughed and interjected:

'We'll scratch a message on the slate by the cave entrance GONE FISHING!'

The men sneak off to go fishing

Eye to eye

While they are all sitting around the fire, the men's conversation flows freely, and there seems to be something about being physically on the same level that reduces people's inhibitions about making conversation.

The phrase 'seeing eye-to-eye' reveals a great deal about the way that people make connections. Nobody is 'above' any of the others and opinions are freely shared across status and generation.

Part of this stems from the fact that they have a common interest and are comfortable to express their opinions. However, what is very revealing is that it works on a physical, horizontal plane. Being on the same level really does make things easier.

Imagine the scenario of a school parents' evening. You're probably milling around looking at the displayed work of the various age groups, waiting your turn to meet your child's teachers. Even though you've never met the people standing around you, you don't find it too difficult to break into conversation. There's a common interest and, once again, you're on the same level.

The same bond connects a group of expectant mothers sitting around at an ante-natal class and as for men ... they can walk into any American sports bar or British pub, lean on the counter and talk football. Admittedly they won't be talking about the same game in those two locations, but even a fleeting knowledge of the local teams will enable them to strike up a conversation easily.

All being on the same level, and all having a common connection, effectively reduces the fear of exposure and it is this fear of exposure that encourages the butterflies to invade.

Consider an example that you've probably come across at one time or another. Imagine a meeting at which the chairman asks for comments and questions from the floor. A hand goes up in the fourth row of the audience, and someone starts to raise an issue, speaking with clarity and without any hesitation or self-consciousness.

Then the chairman asks the audience member if they would mind standing up so that the audience can hear more easily. Immediately, panic sets in. The same individual, who was until a few moments ago totally lucid and logical in the points they were raising, is now reduced to flushed embarrassment and struggling to express their opinion.

They're not *on the same level* any longer. The mere fact of being slightly elevated has generated waves of self-consciousness.

It works the other way around, too. If you are a child and the teacher is standing over you, you're more intimidated and nervous than if the teacher is sitting down behind a desk, at the same level as all the students.

One of the smart tricks of the T.G.I. Friday's restaurant chain is that the servers are taught to squat by the table when they take your food and drinks order so that they are on the same level as the customer. It's smart: it's calculated and it creates an informality that really works well in that type of casual-dining restaurant.

Being on the same level actually means more than just the obvious factual observation of the physical situation.

I have tested this with small groups of a dozen participants seated in a U-shaped classroom format. We were able to have an animated conversation, with everyone sitting around and participating. And then, in the middle of the discussion, I would ask the person who was starting to speak to continue the discussion standing up. The result is embarrassment, hesitation, and everything slows down and becomes awkward.

Try it yourself. As you stand up, you will feel your attitude changing. You will feel a weight of responsibility coming on to your shoulders. Your tone of voice will change. You will probably find yourself analysing more deeply what you want to say. You will take time to choose your words more carefully. Certainly there will be a change in your level of confidence.

For some people, the elevation boosts them with an injection of per-ceived authority. For others, the sense of vulnerability is frightening.

Sometimes, you will make a presentation while both you and your audience are seated round the table. Sometimes this is appropriate, but generally you establish your authority by standing to talk. It gives you an additional perceived authority and credibility.

Sidney Lumet's famous movie *Twelve Angry Men* is about a jury con-sidering their verdict at the end of a trial. As you watch the scenes in the jury-room, you can see the effect it has when jurors either remain seated around the table or stand and move about to talk. The dynamics are constantly changing, and this reflects on the impact of the various speakers and the power of their contributions.

129

Speeches and presentations

This sense of distance and separation is a fundamental part of some types of speaking out.

The sermon in a church, mosque or temple is made from an elevated standpoint such as a pulpit. A ruler or monarch traditionally speaks from a throne which embodies their absolute authority. But this book is not about speeches; it's about presentations, and there is an essential difference between the two types of communicating with groups.

A speech-maker speaks with authority that may be either real or perceived. He or she does not expect to be challenged or questioned unless a point needs clarification. A speech will be directive, setting out principles, policies or instructions. A speech is not up for discussion or debate; it is a point of view that comes with the endorsement of the authority that the speaker embodies.

This might be the philosophical and ethical credibility of a religious leader, the political authority of a government official, or the military authority of an officer delivering an operational briefing.

By contrast, a presentation is conversational.

While a speech instructs, a presentation persuades; it leads the audience along, rather than telling them where to go. We will explore this concept of *conversation* in the coming chapters, and contrast it with erroneous approaches and attitudes that can get in the way of clear communication.

Because a presentation incorporates the idea of influence, there is a temptation to overemphasize the importance of tone of voice – a common misconception that Naomi finds particularly confusing.

Image is everything?

Naomi is concerned about her presentation style and seeks help from Uncle James when she meets him once again at the Station Hotel in Anchorford.

'Hello, James. I know you want me to call you James, but I'm still not comfortable with it!'

'Oh but it makes me feel s-o-o much younger, Naomitik.'

'And Naomitik makes me feel as if I'm in short socks again! Anyway, thanks for giving me the opportunity to run through one or two things before the management conference. I want to get some general tips about delivery style.'

'That's no problem at all. Is there anything in particular that's worrying you?'

Naomi sighed and reflected for a moment.

'Yes, there is. And I can't quite sort it out. It's this business about non-verbal communication. I went on a presentation skills course a couple of years ago and then last week I was at a Chamber of Commerce event when once again these trainers were talking about the importance of personal branding and image.'

James smiled.

'Well, that's becoming increasingly important. A few years back, nobody knew who the captains of industry were, and now they've got their own image consultants, press officers and high profiles in TV programmes like The Apprentice *and* Dragons' Den. *You should think about building your own image as a woman finance director, at least in and around the local community.*

'There aren't too many of your breed around, you know.'

Naomi nodded and quickly replied:

'No. I mean – yes, I know all that, and I absolutely do have ambitions in that direction. What's worrying me is not the personal branding stuff: I accept all that. It's that weird percentage all these people bandy around about communication being 93 per cent non-verbal.'

'Ah, yes, that old chestnut. Albert Mehrabian's research in the States. Go on, Naomi, I can guess what you're going to say.'

'Well, it seems everyone who talks about presentations or personal image quotes Mehrabian's research that only seven per cent of our communication is the actual words—'

James interrupted:

'And tone of voice is 38 per cent and body language is 55 per cent. That's what you're about to say isn't it? Well, it's probably one of the most misinterpreted pieces of academic research on the web. Even Professor Mehrabian has tried to correct it on his own website and in Wikipedia but still people get it wrong.'

Naomi beamed in relief as she replied:

'I thought it didn't make sense, but I've heard it time and again. When I left university, I asked an image consultant to do my colours – you know, what suited me and what made me look good. She was the first one I heard talking about Mehrabian, and I must say I blossomed with confidence, because I started to think that what really mattered was – if you like – the packaging more than the contents.

'Once I had my suit and my cream blouse with the red scarf and the right hair-do, I reckoned I was 55 per cent there, and I know I've got a good voice which meant I was 93 per cent there, even if I was talking rubbish!'

'And being an intelligent woman, Naomitik, you reckoned that all that stuff on non-verbal communication didn't make sense?'

'But then there was this research that said that it did!'

James drained his glass and looked around for the barman.

'Let me get you another drink and I'll explain what it's all about and why the content of your presentation is far more important than your body language and tone of voice.'

'I'm all ears. I'm fascinated!'

'Mehrabian's research was about the communication of emotions. *On his website, Mehrabian points out that: "Unless a*

communicator is talking about their feelings or attitudes, these equations are not applicable."

'People have taken this specific research on emotional communication and transposed it to general communication. In doing that, they got it wrong; even so, it's fair to say that a speaker talking about wealth creation needs to look affluent and well-dressed if his message is to be credible.

'All these image consultants and presentation trainers carefully overlook the context of Mehrabian's findings. It's not generally about business communication.

'When you're making a business presentation you're essentially trying to get your audience to change their mindset, and to think and act differently. You're not primarily talking about your feelings and emotions.

'The classic example, to demonstrate what Mehrabian was getting at, is if you were to say to someone: "I want us to be friends" when your body-language and your tone of voice are loud and aggressive, at odds with the words that you are actually using.'

Naomi interrupted:

'Well of course, if you're saying something like that in an aggressive tone, with your fists clenched and your jaw set firm, then it's pretty obvious that you don't mean what you're saying.

'And in the same way, I wouldn't expect anyone to believe me if I was talking about the company's wonderful record-breaking results when we'd downgraded the annual management conference to a meeting in the village hall instead of at a top-class hotel. It would be incongruous.'

James laughed out loud.

'That's precisely the word that Mehrabian uses. It's all about congruence. If your words are not congruent with your tone and your body language, you won't communicate effectively.

> 'So, forget about the 7 per cent – 38 per cent – 55 per cent rule and just remember the word congruent. You can accentuate and emphasize your message by ensuring that your tone of voice and your body language are congruent with the actual words you are using.

> 'In simple terms, congruence means telling the good news with a smile on your face!'

Naomi now looked much more relaxed:

> 'And not making light of serious messages. So, what do you think about wearing my suit and my cream blouse with the red scarf?'

Naomi was teasing her uncle, and he recognized the twinkle in her eye – but chose to give her a straight response:

> 'If that's what the image consultant says is right for you – and more importantly, if that's what makes you feel confident and comfortable – then I'm sure you'll look the part.'

> 'James, you've already made my trip out to Anchorford today more than worthwhile. Thank you so much for sorting that out.'

> 'So, is there anything else that's bugging you, before we get on to catching up about the family?'

Naomi reached for her briefcase and pulled out her notes, together with an A4 folder entitled Handouts.

> 'I took your advice I've simplified the slides, taken off all the super-fluous details and put these into detailed documents that will be on people's chairs when they come into the auditorium, so that they've got all the statistics to hand to refer to when I get to that part of my piece.

> 'Then the handout packs have most of the original source material, together with a Word document that tells the whole story.'

> 'And when will they get those handout packs?'

'*You won't catch me out, James! Those packs are in the follow-up material which all the delegates will find in their hotel rooms at the end of the day, when they go to change for the gala dinner. All I have to do now is get my performance right.*'

Although Naomi gave James a big, proud, friendly smile, she was met with a blank stare.

Then James replied:

'*Well, young lady, I hope not.*'

'*Hope not … what? I don't understand, James, I really want it to go well next week and that's why I've come to you for advice.*'

'*Yes, Naomi, but you said* performance. *You said you want to "get your performance right". Big mistake! Now, let me explain.*'

'*In my time I've seen many senior executives take the stage and give a "performance". They wanted to put on a show, and some of them proved to be great entertainers.*'

James continued:

'*But very few, if any, business presentations are primarily about "entertaining" your audience. Your presentation, as we said at the outset, is all about getting people to change their mindset about the company performance.*'

'*I know, I know, James – but if I don't come across in the right way, then nothing will ever change. Look, I'm a woman in what has always been a man's job at this company. It's the first time they've all met me and—*'

James quickly interrupted:

'*Hold it right there! That's what we're talking about. Now you're using the right language. Did you hear what you just said? You said: "It's the first time they've all met me." This is what it's all about. They are meeting you and you're going to have a* conversation *with them.*

135

'*And before you object, let me assure you that it's perfectly possible to have a conversation with a couple of hundred people. It's all about style of delivery and tone of voice.*

'*You are not an orator addressing a vast crowd, like Winston Churchill making one of his wartime radio broadcasts. Nor are you Martin Luther King calling for revolutionary social change, nor Nelson Mandela welcoming the birth of the "Rainbow Nation" of the new South Africa.*

'*Major occasions like those call for orators in what is essentially a one-way communication. Presentations, on the other hand, call for dialogue.*

'*Even though your audience are not going to interact with you openly, you will be having an imaginary conversation with them. They will not respond vocally – but they may respond with a smile and a nod that show they are listening, thinking and interacting with you, in exactly the same way as if you were meeting in a coffee shop or propping up the bar in the local pub.*

'*However, whereas delivering a great speech as an orator demands that you* perform, *having a conversation means that you have to* relax. *And that means you must be in your comfort zone.*

'*That's not so simple when you're in a strange environment and nervous about what you have to do. So, the first thing to do is establish your personal comfort zone so that you come across as being confident and convincing.*

'*We can talk about that comfort zone and then, when we talk about being on-stage, we can look at how you keep that conversational tone.*'

James ordered another round and then moved on to explain the basic principles of advance preparation and how to keep on track with what you want to say.

Making lists

Lists are a way of putting your mind at rest.

As you tick things off the list, you have one less thing to worry about. It doesn't matter whether you're preparing for a shopping trip, a holiday, a DIY project or a business presentation; the most organized and least stressful way to start is with a list.

Some of the topics on the list will be general preparation, some will relate specifically to the presentation itself, and other items will be about personal and last-minute things you need to attend to.

What are you worried about?

There is nothing rational about the way that you feel – but knowing this doesn't make the nervous panic go away.

You may be afraid of stammering, of blushing, of shaking, of drying up and not being able to speak. You may even be afraid of fainting with fright! You may well know that you have done all your preparation and that you have thought about and prepared for every eventuality – but still you are worried.

So, how can you cope with fears that are totally irrational?

The answer is that the only thing that will get you out of this negative spiral is facing up to it and doing it.

There are comparable fears that are similarly irrational, like the fear of flying. Some people have decided that they can never board an aircraft, even for a short flight. No matter what the safety statistics say, they are incapable of overcoming their belief that something terrible will happen and they will fall out of the sky. They will never change their mind unless they take the risk and do it.

It will take something dramatic – like one of your children emigrating to Australia and producing your first grandchild – that will create the motive for taking the plunge and overcoming your fear. The fear is real and debilitating, just as psychosomatic illness is totally real and debilitating.

Practice really does make perfect

With practice, it gets easier, and there are many opportunities for learning to speak in public through practice.

In particular, Toastmasters International (http://www.toastmasters .org) offers a warm welcome to new members and has an outstanding educational programme at a fraction of the cost of commercial programmes.

Toastmasters International has nothing to do with men in red coats acting as master-of-ceremonies at weddings. The men in red coats come from various separate organizations that operate under the Toastmasters' General Council.

By contrast, Toastmasters International is a global organization. Its UK division has expanded rapidly in recent years, and thrives with clubs in many towns across Britain and Ireland.

Guests are always welcomed warmly, and while there is never any pressure to move more quickly than you wish, you will be supported to move out of your comfort zone when you are ready. Most clubs have a broad range of members – from some who are facing up to their fear of public speaking, through to others who earn their living as managers or trainers and want to improve their professional skills.

The golden rule that comes through the basic training programme of Toastmasters is the importance of preparation.

Remember that the main reason the butterflies are giving you acute indigestion is because there is detailed preparation that needs attending to. The more time and effort you put into ensuring that you are well-prepared, the easier the presentation becomes.

Then you can concentrate on the actual delivery of what you want to say.

And the extent to which you know exactly what you are going to say will depend on how much of your presentation is going to be pre-determined and verbatim, and how much is going to be off-the-cuff. Which you choose is a matter of personal preference and experience.

Either way, there are two schools of thought about how much last-minute preparation will help you to look relaxed and confident – and how much will make you look like a preprogrammed automaton.

Reading line-by-line or learning word for word

Some speakers rehearse endlessly until they are word perfect.

I know one speaker who perfected the art of delivering his speech synchronized to a recording he made, and played from a device in his pocket connected with a fine flex to a miniature earpiece. I cannot vouch for how well this worked as I never saw him actually speak this way from the platform – but I cannot imagine that the audience would feel his words were genuine.

I've watched several outstanding speakers deliver their standard speech on two or three consecutive occasions; I have heard the same jokes and pauses, and watched the same movements and gestures. It works for them, and the audience seem to like it, but my own opinion is that it comes at the cost of any sense of spontaneity.

Working from a script

Some speakers like to read their speech.

When you are standing at a lectern and intend to read a print-out of what you plan to say, be sure that you produce your final copy in a clear font that is easy to read. If you normally wear reading-glasses, you will need to decide whether you will be wearing them for your presentation, or whether you will make the font extra-large.

I personally have the opposite problem, as I do not wear spectacles for reading or computer work, but do wear them for driving and distance. Consequently, I tend not to wear them when I'm facilitating an event on-stage and will need to refer to notes. You need to work out what you are comfortable with.

If you are speaking at a major conference, there may be an autocue (tele-prompt) system. The way this works is that your presentation is taken as a Word document and loaded into a computer, which then formats it into a large font, wide spaced, together with notes to warn you when there are different visuals or video clips as Audience Support.

This text appears on a monitor screen in front of you, and an operator manually scrolls through your script as you read it, so that you can read your presentation line by line. At major events, the organizers may position two or three monitors at strategic points on the platform – or even project the text on to the back wall of the room – so that you can move around and not be seen to be obviously reading from a prepared script.

Is autocue the answer?

Autocue is a good solution when the words you speak have to be exactly the same as the words on the press release or post-meeting handouts.

Hence, it's ideal for corporate AGMs and for politicians delivering policy statements.

Some executives like to use autocue at management conferences. In my experience however it cramps style and leads to a stilted style of delivery. It's very difficult to develop a conversational style if you are using a prepared presentation and delivering it verbatim.

Working from autocue needs training, especially in developing trust between you and the autocue operator who is scrolling your text as you are speaking.

There are various techniques you can learn that will help you keep a steady flow to your speaking – but above all it's a matter of practice. Make sure you get plenty of that before you deliver your first presentation from autocue.

With or without notes

Some speakers like to go to the other extreme and aim for total spontaneity.

They know their subject inside out. Having prepared a series of visuals that will cover the various points that they want to make, they talk in a casual and informal way, using the visuals to keep them on track.

There is a danger when the Audience Support is used as Speaker Support in this way, as you learned earlier. You must be confident that what goes on the screen leads the audience through your story, and not that you have to translate and explain what appears.

When you tell your story, it's generally better to work from a synopsis of the story itself rather than from the pictures that illustrate it. It's back once more to the Seventh Commandment of PowerPoint – Separate *speaker support* from *audience support* – and be clear in your mind what that means.

Look at your material and ask yourself this simple question: '*Who does this visual help – me or the audience*?'

Create your cue cards

This is often the best way to talk to an audience.

You can achieve the effect of being spontaneous and confident if you go for the ideal solution of jotting down the key milestones of your speech and having these as your notes.

On one occasion recently, I was asked to stand in at just an hour's notice when a speaker failed to arrive for an event. I quickly jotted down some headings that would give me the bare bones of a structure and then delivered a 45 minute presentation which, I have to admit, was probably better than one I might have given with a few days' preparation.

I put a couple of sheets of A4 paper on the lectern that was at the side of the platform then spoke from centre stage, moving around freely, and from time to time glancing over at my notes to check that I was still on track, and what my next point was.

My preferred approach is to work out the structure and outline of a speech, much as Section One describes, and then to reduce the sections to 3 x 5 index cards which I can have as prompts.

If you use this method, leave the top card blank for notes of any last-minute additions to your opening remarks, and remember to number the cards and join them together with a corded treasury tag. Then, if you drop your cue cards you can simply pick them up with the relief of knowing that the treasury tag ensures that they will have stayed in the right order!

Do remember that this isn't Shakespeare and the audience don't have a copy of the script. When you go to the theatre to see a performance of a classical play, there are certain lines that you expect to hear; and if the actors get it wrong you will probably be critical of their errors.

You don't have that problem with your presentation, because the audience don't know what you're going to say. Remind yourself that you're having a *conversation*, not delivering a *speech*. They won't know if you forget your lines and say something differently from the way you had originally planned.

On the hoof and off the cuff

Some people have the ability to talk spontaneously: to take any subject and express an opinion simply and clearly. There are also people who *think* they have this ability, but frankly don't.

Even if you don't intend to use notes, and even if you have talked on this particular subject many times before, I would recommend that you make a habit of drafting an outline and jotting down a few headings before you speak. It will help to clear your mind, to rank and arrange your points and also to remind you of any thoughts and reactions that may have arisen the last time you gave this particular presentation.

You can then fold up the paper and put it in your pocket or handbag; you don't have to use it as a reference, but you will certainly find that making a few notes will help to focus your thoughts on what you are going to say.

Summary

Eye to eye

A good presentation meets people on their own level and has the feel and quality of a conversation. Whereas a *speech* seeks to *instruct* the audience, a *presentation* seeks to *persuade and influence*.

The single most important thing about your presentation is what you have to say: the story you want to tell and the content that supports your story.

Albert Mehrabian's much-quoted research must be taken in context. It is not true that communication is only 7 per cent content and 93 per cent voice and body language.

What his research does demonstrate is the need for congruence in emotional communication between what you say, your tone of voice and your body language. While Mehrabian's research dealt primarily with emotions, the principle still holds good. You will send out confusing and mixed messages if you are saying one thing and acting as if you mean something else.

Make a list of everything you need to do in advance; nothing is more satisfying than ticking off the various elements of your preparation.

Work out whether you need to deliver your presentation verbatim – as you may have to if it has to be available in print as a handout – or whether you can condense your words to cue cards and adopt a less formal approach.

With cue cards, leave the top one blank and join the cards with a treasury tag so they always stay in the correct order.

10

Creating your comfort zone

The right environment

So much for the content of the presentation and how you will help it along; now, what about the setting – the room in which this is all going to take place?

It doesn't matter whether it's a small meeting room in your offices or an international conference centre; whatever the location, you need to familiarize yourself with the layout and practical details.

Sometimes you get to choose how, when and where you are presenting. At other times it may all be pre-arranged and you have to fit in with arrangements that have already been finalized. Either way, you want to make the location work to your advantage as much as possible.

Create your environment

Where you have the choice of setting the time and place – as you might for an internal presentation – don't schedule it for first thing in the morning, when people are still thinking about their emails and everything else that they have to do that day; nor straight after lunch when they are slightly drowsy.

Friday afternoon meetings can work for you or against you. There is something to be said for pushing through new ideas on a Friday, when people's minds are drifting towards the weekend and they might want to get the meeting over and settled. On the other hand, you may not have people's full attention when their minds are elsewhere.

Where the occasion is a presentation to a small group, use a room that is neither too small for comfort nor too large and likely to inhibit good communication. Position yourself away from the door, to minimize the effect of any interruptions should anyone need to leave in the course of the meeting, or if someone might be joining you at a later stage.

In addition, you should give some thought not only to where you will speak from but also to where you will sit afterwards.

Check out the venue

When it's a major event in a conference environment, the amount of flexibility that you will have to change what has been arranged will depend very much on the size of the event and the expertise of the organizers.

Large-scale events are usually put together by a team of professionals, sometimes with a production capability on the scale of a major television show. At other times, the duty manager at the hotel might simply have asked the overnight staff to put out some chairs, without any forethought as to how to create the best layout.

Sometimes you might find that the seating has been set out so that the front row is a long way back from the platform, which is very isolating for the speakers. At other times, they might have left a very wide central gangway which means that speakers will be talking into a void.

It may be that you have to put up with what you are given, but as long as you make a point of checking the room in advance then you will avoid any unwelcome surprises at the last minute.

Check the 'alities'

Whatever the room, there are certain basics that should be on your checklist:

> Technicality
> Practicality
> Hospitality

Get the technology right

Whether your presentation is high-tech or low-tech, make sure you allow time to run through it on-site.

Even if you expect to deliver the presentation from your own laptop, make sure you bring an extra copy on a memory stick or CD-ROM (or both!) just in case something goes wrong.

Many small meeting rooms are now fully equipped with a data-projector – a *beamer*, as they are sometimes called. What could be easier than to arrive and simply plug your laptop into the venue's projector?

Well, it's not always that easy. While technology improves month by month, there are still frequent difficulties in getting two items of hardware to talk to each other. Make sure you allow extra time for this. If you don't need the extra time, you can relax for those precious minutes instead.

Some conferences are set up to run all the presentations from one backstage PC. The operator advances your slides on a signal that you control from a button on the lectern or a remote control.

Where your presentation is to be loaded onto their computer, you'll do well to check in advance that you are running the same version of PowerPoint, just to ensure that there are no glitches caused by conflicting versions of the software. As long as you leave time to sort this out once you get to the venue, then a competent technician will be able to sort out your material to match the other presentations if there is any difference in format.

However, if you're running your presentation from your own laptop you'll probably find it worth investing in a remote control to advance your PowerPoint. A spare battery is essential for this – especially if you don't use the clicker very often!

A well-organized large-scale event will usually have a technical run-through in advance. This is not so that you can practise your words; it's to ensure that the PowerPoint runs smoothly, that your microphone works, and that you're not either standing in a shadow or blinded by a spotlight.

Make sure you are comfortable with the arrangements that are finalized in this session. Later could be too late!

Check out the practical details

When you are running a session alone, and don't have to consider the whims and preferences of any other speakers, start by arranging the furniture the way you would like it. Move the tables and chairs around. Place the laptop and projector where you want them. Once you've moved the equipment, check that it's still working efficiently and that you haven't unplugged or disconnected anything,

Where you are speaking from a platform, check out the lectern. Is there a shelf where you can put a glass of water, a pack of tissues or any props that you may need? Are you able to put anything in place in preparation, so you don't need to bring it up with you later? And have you ensured that nobody will tidy it away without realizing that you've just put it there?

When you are working with a small audience, you may be using a flip chart – especially useful when your presentation is intended to be interactive and you want feedback that you can note down and refer to later. Make sure you position the flip chart on the correct side. If you are right-handed, then you want the easel on the left hand side of the stage (looking from where you are on the stage) so that you don't have to cross in front of it to write anything.

And if you're using a laptop and data projector, organize the front of the room so that you don't have to walk across the beam of light. It's just as important to check out the basics, such as flip charts, as it is to check out the more technological equipment. Although hotels pride themselves in providing flip charts and pens, any trainer will tell you that all of these faults are common:

1. The pens are dried out.
2. Much of the flip chart pad has been used so you don't have sufficient blank pages.
3. The clips to hold the pad are broken.
4. The legs of the flip-chart stand are unstable, threatening to collapse just as you start to write.

Whenever you are using flip charts, bring your own pens as back-up and check out both the easels and the pads well before your session is due to start.

The same goes for overhead projectors. Although OHPs are less commonly used these days, with most people preferring the integrated solution offered by PowerPoint and laptop computers, they are still an easy, low-tech way to work with a small group.

Again, check the equipment if it is being provided for you, and when bringing your own make sure you have both a spare fuse and a spare lamp.

Points like this are partly a matter of professionalism. However, they are also a matter of self-interest: if something goes wrong you run the likelihood of being 'thrown' by the incident and losing a degree of confidence. Just do everything you can to make your life easier by checking and double-checking in advance.

Clock-watching

The French monarch, Louis XVIII, coined the saying '*Punctuality is the courtesy of kings*'.

Being regal in your presentation skills can be difficult. So, how can you ensure that you keep to time without becoming obsessive and losing the spirit and flow of your presentation? How do you keep an eye on the time?

Generally, clock-watching is frowned on in the corporate environment. In the context of presentations, however, it is a much-valued virtue. But can you see the clock – and does it tell the right time?

Nothing is more distracting than speakers who frequently glance down at their wristwatch.

When the speaker does it, the audience takes the visual clue and they all do the same.

As a speaker, you'll find few things more disconcerting than seeing the entire audience looking down at their wristwatches.

Get yourself one of those small battery-powered travel alarm clocks that you can buy for a pound or two, and put it on the lectern or desk when you check the arrangements. Nobody will know that you're keeping an eye on the time, so they won't be doing so themselves.

It's a cheap and easy trick of the trade. Just make sure you turn OFF the alarm function!

Be a good host – and look after yourself, too

Where it's a small meeting, and your audience are also your guests, you must check on the hospitality that is arranged.

At the very least you will have water on the table, and possibly hot beverages or cold drinks too.

Where it is to be a long session, you may require other refreshments – so let me give you a word of caution. While much of continental Europe still holds to the civilized concept of a proper break for a meal at lunchtimes, many businesses and organizations in the UK and North America work through and have a snack sent in.

This can create a hiatus in the mood of the room, and make it difficult to carry on with the theme of the presentation.

When you are to have a presentation over the lunch period, aim to have the presentation first, then handle any immediate questions, and then continue in a more informal context while everyone tucks into the sandwiches.

You will not have everyone's full attention while they are eating, watching and listening – and at the same time wondering if there's any mustard on the table, and trying to avoid getting mayonnaise down the front of their outfit. Your presentation should stimulate their appetite, both for more information and for their lunch.

Write your own introduction

When it's a big occasion and there is a host or facilitator who will introduce you, it's important to ensure that the audience is favourably disposed.

You don't necessarily want a big build-up, but you want the audience to be sufficiently interested in your imminent appearance so that they'll give you a fighting chance of winning their respect and admiration. If you are irresponsibly modest about this, you may well find yourself swimming against the stream to overcome the negative effect of a lukewarm or indifferent introduction.

Often the chairman would appreciate your help on how you would like to be introduced – and if you don't help him or her out, you could find that both you and the audience will get off on the wrong foot.

So write out your introduction, word-for-word, in a clear, sans-serif font (such as Arial or Trebuchet), enlarged to 16 point, and print it out wide-spaced on one A4 sheet.

The chairman will then introduce you without the risk of getting any of the facts wrong, he or she won't pre-empt any of the key points that you want to make, and the audience will hear just what you want them to hear: no more and no less.

What's more, the chairman will be grateful to you for providing a clear, concise and easy-to-read script.

It's called *edification*. To edify is 'to benefit spiritually' and because it's a transitive verb, it's almost like giving a blessing. That's what the chairman will do for you: a gentle build-up. It's the precise opposite of the urban slang verb to 'diss', which means to heap disrespect onto someone and actively put them down.

Without being condescending or patronizing, you should make a point of edifying the speakers who have preceded you, together with the sponsors of the event and the audience. The rule here is modesty and humility. Yes, there's a fine line between edification and veering over towards ingratiation, but common sense will guide you not to overdo it.

Just one cultural caveat: as a rule, Europeans in America should over-edify and Americans in Europe should under-edify. There will be more about cultural differences and paralanguage barriers later in the book.

Dressing for the occasion

I have facilitated many management and sales conferences where nobody really gave any thought to what the dress-code should be. Although the invitation might have stated 'Business Casual', people had generally put their own interpretation on it and the result was that nobody was entirely comfortable.

On one occasion, the CEO arrived early in the morning of an event for a final run-through, to find all the men in his management team in suits and ties. He immediately decided that this looked too formal and ordered ties to be removed.

The result was a team who looked like a group of electioneering politicians, trying to establish their City credibility by wearing suits, while still maintaining their *street cred* by not wearing ties.

There is also the matter of respecting your audience. When you are speaking overseas, you must be aware of the traditions and expectations of your host country.

Many countries expect more formality than would be the norm in the UK, and in the US men may still come across the culture of *dark suit, white shirt and tie with a fleck of red* that once epitomized the American corporate culture.

Certainly, men won't go wrong if they choose that option ... but men ... do empty your pockets except, perhaps, for a tissue or handkerchief. Your clothes will look smarter and you won't have keys or small change jingling as you move around the stage.

As a man I find it difficult to find the balance in that confusing phrase *smart casual* and I know that many women face the same dilemma. The single most important rule for everyone is to respect the culture of your audience, particularly in countries with a strong religious tradition.

Far be it from me to tell a woman what to wear – that's got me into too much trouble in the past! All that I would say is a word of warning about jewellery: it can be distracting.

Be *comfortable*. That's the golden rule for both men and women. If in doubt, it is generally better to be over-dressed than under-dressed. You can get away with being slightly more formal than anyone else, on the grounds that you are there with a particular role to fulfil.

Summary

Bits and pieces

Butterflies are the result of fear. Some of that fear stems from a dread that something unexpected and unavoidable will sabotage all your efforts – this can be diminished with thorough preparation.

Other fears may be completely irrational but will ultimately decline if you bite the bullet and create opportunities for practice and experimentation. It's like riding Nemesis at Alton Towers, or learning to ride a bicycle or roller-skates: the only way to conquer the fear is to do it.

Assuming you have followed the recommendations in the first two sections of this book, then you've done everything you can to ensure that you've minimized the risks that stem from a lack of preparation.

You know your topic and your story. You've prepared whatever notes, visual aids and other materials that you might need. You've checked out the room, the layout and the seating. You've familiarized yourself with the platform and the technology, and you're dressed to look the part.

Well, you've handled all the external stuff and created the essentials for your own comfort zone. So, what's going on inside?

For some people, the butterflies will still bring a terrifying fear of failure; everyone has something that pushes their buttons. The butterflies are still there, even if your planning and organization do mean that they're now flying in formation. You are anxious, you're nervous and maybe even worried.

How do you handle this?

11

It's good to be nervous

The fear is real – it's OK to be very afraid

If you have made your lists, and gone through ticking things off, then the panic must have diminished to some extent, simply because there are now fewer uncertainties.

For some people, and I include myself in this, that's about as comforting as wearing a safety helmet before buckling up for a bungee jump.

I once took a personal development course that involved white-water rafting, which I absolutely adored, and high-wire walking, which terrified me. I remember climbing ten metres up the rungs that were driven into a tall tree, and then I froze, halfway up, unable to move. I was wearing a full harness which was attached to a rope and pulleys controlled by two colleagues, so there was no way that I could fall. Nevertheless, I was locked solid and unable to move either up or down.

Then, with shouts of encouragement ringing in my ears, I suddenly took off and climbed up and across the high wire, tears of relief and amazement in my eyes.

Once my brain had done the logical analysis and established that I was perfectly safe, I could negate my fears and complete the exercise.

154

This process doesn't always happen instantly. It is only in relatively recent years that children have been able to overcome an instinctive fear of water by having the *opportunity* to visit warm, indoor swimming pools.

I remember my own childhood experiences were in freezing outdoor pools. As long as the water temperature was above 13 degrees Celsius it was deemed warm enough for us to learn to swim. At 13 degrees it was difficult to breathe, because our teeth wouldn't stop chattering from the cold. Putting our faces under water felt like a near-death experience.

Looking back on it now, I think our fears of imminent heart failure were almost justified and I can still remember being so cold that the teachers never had to tell us to stop talking: we couldn't speak or fool around as it was difficult enough just breathing.

When you're scared, it doesn't really help if someone tells you that your fear is irrational. You have to handle it yourself, just as I had to, up there on the high wire in the forest.

Ask any professional speaker how they manage to look so calm and collected when they are addressing an audience and they will tell you that it's duck syndrome. From what everyone can see they are like a duck, gliding along serenely; but beneath the surface of the water their feet are paddling furiously. The cool and calm exterior hides a brain that is working flat out to hold an orderly structure, keep the body breathing steadily to project a good, solid tone of voice and at the same time, desperately trying to remember to smile.

When you are not prepared, there is logical reason to be anxious – but even then, you can in time acquire the skill to think on your feet and speak without preparation. Practice doesn't just make perfect; it's practice that gets you from amateur to average, and from average to excellent.

The difference between stress and strain

Thank goodness I can still feel those nerves each time I am in front of an audience! The day you are not nervous is the day you should start to worry.

Nerves are a sign that you are taking things seriously; if you're not nervous, you're probably going to come across as being arrogant, which is a sure way to distance yourself from your audience. Don't fall into that trap!

Watch politicians when they are being interviewed and decide for yourself whether you would rather come across with arrogance or with sincerity. You'll see plenty of examples in interviews and you can draw your own conclusions.

I once had to write a speech for a newly-appointed senior executive, who was addressing a group of a couple of hundred managers for the first time. In person, he came across as superbly confident and briefed me in no uncertain terms as to what he wanted to say:

> *'I want you to give me plenty of that humility stuff. You know the sort of thing. Lines like: "You guys here today have forgotten more about this industry than I can hope to learn while I head up this division."'*

Such words may sound modest, but when they are delivered with a degree of bravado the sentiment is pretty transparent. He was right in assessing how long he would have to learn about the business. His tone didn't go down well with a skilled and experienced team of colleagues, and within six months he had been replaced by someone with a more sensitive approach.

There is a lot of talk about *stress management* and the need to reduce stress in the workplace. Perhaps it's just semantics, but I want to make the point that *stress* is good – whereas obsessive anxiety leads to *strain*.

Strain impedes action, and the tension and worry can be damaging. Without stress there would be no competition, no new records of achievement or exploration. The Olympics would be like *Chariots of Fire*, when competitive sport was relaxed and laid-back and recreational, with hardly a whisper of professionalism.

It's the *stress*, that people such as Steve Redgrave and Kelly Holmes put into their physical endeavours, that enables them to break the records and bring home the gold medals; while *strain* will only block you and hold you back.

156

Perhaps society did lose something when we started to turn 'games' into serious competition – but you owe it to your audience to respect their commitment to you. You are a valuable commodity and you owe it to yourself. Look at the figures.

Value for money

Where you are talking for half an hour to a group of a dozen executives, do a quick calculation of the wages being paid out for those people to be at that presentation. When you are addressing a major conference, you will appreciate that the sums involved soon become astronomic.

That's the value that is being put on you, and you have a duty to deliver that value. It is irresponsible not to take a presentation seriously. All that stress and those associated nerves are a healthy sign that you understand the importance of the opportunity and the occasion.

Just like the athlete stretching her legs and jogging to the starting line, or like the oarsman stretching his shoulders as he grips the blade, you should feel the stress and know that you are focused on doing what you have to do. The secret is in not letting the stress turn into strain.

Now you must use the healthy tension of being focused and tuned in to your objective, without letting it develop into the strain of panic or anxiety.

Last-minute nerves

You don't need to be anxious. Look at the facts: you've done all the preparation, you're satisfied with your story and all the support you need to illustrate it. You've checked out the room and all the arrangements, and you're looking good. Now all you need is five minutes of quiet, and you know just where you can find that.

Switching off and tuning in

There's more than one reason for a last-minute visit to the washroom, so give yourself five minutes of absolute privacy in the smallest room, to get yourself into the right frame of mind.

A few years ago the idea of meditation would have been unthinkable in the business context – but since most of today's senior executives were growing up during the 'hippie' era, attitudes have broadened. 'Switching off and tuning in' are no longer the exclusive preserve of New Age thinkers.

What you are going to do is find the inner peace that will replace the tension and anxiety that may currently be occupying your mind. There's nothing weird or 'touchy-feely' about doing this.

Just watch a concert pianist about to perform a difficult solo, or any diver, standing on the high board and about to execute a back one-and-a-half flip. You'll see them settle and ground themselves, clear the mind, and focus. Then they'll flow into a seamless delivery, which is what you'll be able to do with a little practice.

Here are a few tips, in case you're not familiar with 'switching off and tuning in'.

Sit quietly, with your feet flat on the ground. Close your eyes and take a moment to settle, then open up your chest and drop your shoulders down to release any tension. Breathe deeply, in through the nose, then deep down into your lungs, and then exhale gently through the mouth. Do this three times and then let any remaining tension flow out of your body.

Now, take time to visualize what is going to happen – you may find it easier to keep your eyes closed while doing this. Play the scenario through in your mind's eye, exactly as you want it to unfold.

Think of the moments immediately before you begin to speak, and focus on the faces of the people you will be talking to. Imagine the open expressions on their faces, and see them as people who are keen to hear what you want to share with them. Remember why you are speaking, and remind yourself of the way in which you are planning to change the mindset of your audience. When you are comfortable with this thought, take another deep breath and then leave the cubicle.

How well do you know yourself? Go over and take a good look at yourself in the mirror. Look into your eyes and pause a moment. You probably don't do this very often, so take a moment to connect with the real person, and not just with the lipstick and eyebrows or the way your tie is knotted.

By following this simple process, you can establish your mindset for the next hour or so. This is how you identify yourself totally with your inner self, with the person and the character who will be connecting with the audience. In a moment of total privacy, you can have an unspoken conversation with the face in the mirror: you can remind that person of all the work that's gone into the presentation you are about to deliver, and you can congratulate that person on a job well done.

And now you'll be ready to face the music.

Don't let yourself slip into the habit of taking short, shallow breaths, and at the same time don't breathe too deeply or you'll over-oxygenate and become dizzy. Just keep taking steady breaths; this will not only exercise your lungs, it will also help your posture and general confidence.

By following these simple steps, you'll go a long way towards dealing with those butterflies – before you know it you'll be watching yourself in full flow. It's a strange sensation. When you are completely in your own skin and connected with your message, you won't just be the star of your own show; you'll also have a sense of being detached from the nervous person who has been worrying about speaking out.

Sometimes I can almost stand back and hear myself speaking, rather than be the person who is up there delivering the presentation. It's all about living in the moment and being real, being nervous to the point of being carefully conscientious about doing the best possible job.

And you don't need to be alone when you're out there, as Grunt came to discover when he discussed this with Tork, who gave him some basic coaching and encouragement.

You have a friend out there

Grunt was now clear on the story he would be telling, and had worked out how he was going to use various props to help illustrate the points he wanted to make. But he was still nervous:

> *'It's all very well when I'm chatting to you, Tork. But if I've got to stand up in front of the whole village I'm frightened that I won't be able to do it. My knees will be knocking and I'll dry up!'*

> *'Well, suppose I sit somewhere in the middle of the group on one side, and suppose Natter sits somewhere on the other side, and instead of trying to talk to everyone, you can just talk to us. How does that sound?'*

Grunt, thought for a moment, then added:

It helps to have a friend giving you encouragement

'And if I could pick out Alto somewhere in the crowd, and your missus too, then I suppose I could pretend I was just talking to them. That sounds a lot easier. What if nobody can hear me, though? '

'I'll tell you what I'll do: I'll dip my head and put my hand behind my ear, so you'll know to speak up. And if you're doing well I'll give you a great big smile.'

'You know, Tork, I'm beginning to think that might work, after all.'

Summary

Nerves and anticipation

Don't let nerves upset you – instead, be concerned if you're not apprehensive about facing your audience.

Remember that all good professional speakers feel nervous. Remember that you've done all your preparation and that you know your subject. Most importantly, remember that if you exude over-confidence and bravado, you will probably come across as insincere or arrogant, which would be far worse than appearing a little hesitant or apprehensive.

Give yourself five minutes of solitude before you speak. Don't be embarrassed about this; it's no different from the preparation that would be expected from an athlete or a performer.

Remember that breathing is the secret of life! And apart from the fact that you won't live long if you stop, remember that deep, conscious breaths help you concentrate and focus on the job in hand.

12

On your feet

Connection or charisma

When you are communicating with a group you will generally seek to achieve a good level of connection and a degree of familiarity; the latter will vary according to the nature of your relationship with the audience, and also the nature of the occasion.

When you are all on the same level, socially, physically and intellectually – like Grunt and his friends sitting around the fire discussing the manifesto – it's easy to have a conversation. You hear easily and you can listen easily: you connect.

However, in some circumstances you might want to keep a certain distance. If you are a politician or a celebrity, then you need to maintain a charisma because you want to give a performance – and performances need a particular kind of magic.

Celebrities and politicians know all about the importance of anticipation and mystery.

Novelist Thomas Mann's famous story *Mario and the Magician* is an allegory of the way that a political dictator controls his people, distancing himself and establishing an awesome personal authority. The story describes how the central character is a stage hypnotist who keeps the audience waiting for hours, manipulating them by creating tension and anxiety.

Of course there is literary licence in this exaggerated representation of the way things work. But it is true that speakers, trainers, teachers, presenters all have power over their audience if they choose to use it.

This technique – building up the audience's expectations and excitement – is a stock-in-trade of the entertainment business. Pop stars establish their charisma by having other performers appear before them so that by the time the second half of the show starts the audience is full of anticipation for the main attraction. When the superstar finally takes the stage, her or his importance has been established and the audience has been primed.

Making your communication a conversation

It is unlikely that you will be reading this introductory book if you expect a thunderous round of applause as you take the platform, or stand up in front of a dozen co-workers to talk about a new policy on Health and Safety.

Probably you want to be seen as a colleague who intends to share some thoughts and ideas – with the overall intention of changing the mindset of the group or audience.

So, with that in mind, are you going to give a *performance* or are you going to have a *conversation* with your audience?

Some speakers will argue about this, and Stateside you'll see that presentations are far more performance and entertainment orientated than they are in Europe. Much will depend on your own style and personality – but as a general rule it is my suggestion that a conversation is more engaging and more connecting than a performance. What you are trying to do, in order to be persuasive and influential, is be just that – engaging and connecting.

Having a conversation with a small group of acquaintances is one thing, but you're probably wondering how you can have a conversation with a crowd, just as Naomi was discussing with James earlier.

It isn't as difficult as it sounds at first.

Of course, you can't literally chat with each and every individual. However, you can make a sufficient number of personal connections to ensure that you give the impression of a certain degree of personal closeness.

You achieve this by making a point of circulating beforehand and introducing yourself to as many people as possible. It's a walk-about, it's hand-shaking and making small-talk. You're not proselytizing your Big Message; you keep that until your actual presentation. The purpose of this pre-meeting is to put both you and your audience at ease, and to establish some initial connections so that when you speak, you will find that there are one or two faces out there smiling back in acknowledgement.

Ten minutes previously they'd been talking to you about children's school holidays, or whether the local soccer team would be up for promotion this season, or whatever. They feel that they've got to know you a little bit; similarly, you will feel that you have some degree of connection with them.

In addition to this, it's worth having a couple of colleagues out in the audience, as Tork recommended to Grunt. You should arrange in advance that they'll give you feedback, laugh at your jokes or – at least – just be a friendly face.

When I'm speaking at an event with a colleague from the Professional Speakers Association, we will arrange to watch each other's sessions critically and then, over a drink afterwards, we'll pass on our comments and suggestions. I have found that this is the only way to get genuine feedback.

It may boost your ego to have feedback like 'You were excellent' or 'That was really good!' but it's not as helpful as remarks like 'You're not pausing enough to let them take in your key points' or 'Do you realize how often you fiddle with your necktie?'

Claim the stage

There's a simple trick of the trade that will help you to set the tone of your presentation, and it's called claiming the stage.

Let's illustrate this by contrasting Martin, who is making a sales presentation to a small group, and Naomi, who has been asked to speak at the local Women in Business networking event on the effect of proposed taxation changes on capital investment.

We'll assume that Martin has prepared the room and his presentation, and that all the guests have arrived and been offered coffee. Martin starts:

> *'Well, thank you all for coming today. I'm sorry the weather's been so awful for your journey over. I know you're all busy people and – oh, I'm sorry David, let me pass you the milk.'*

One of the guests, David, has been looking for the jug of milk to put in his coffee. Martin pauses to pass it over.

> *'There; I'm afraid it's skimmed, I do hope that's all right. I'm afraid the girls in the office always seem to be dieting – you know how it is. Is skimmed all right for you?'*

David is slightly embarrassed at the fuss Martin is making,

> *'Absolutely fine, Martin. Please don't worry.'*

Martin continues:

> *'Well, if you're quite sure. Let me see, ah yes. It's good to see you all here. I want to talk to you about the new products that we'll be exhibiting next week at Birmingham. We wanted to give you a sneak preview, so it's really good that you can make it. I hope you all managed to find a parking space ...*

And so he goes on:

> *'I've got a few slides. They're not very clear, I'm afraid, but they should give you a rough idea. So, anyway, let me start by looking at what's been happening in the marketplace ...'*

You've been to presentations like that: occasions when presenters have thought that they might reduce their own nervousness and embarrassment by sharing it with the audience.

Their sense of inadequacy leads them into an endless string of apologies for everything – even the wet weather! No, it's *not* polite to keep apologizing! It makes your guests uncomfortable, and that is definitely not the right thing to do.

You won't reduce your own nerves by sharing them with the audience – and you'll create a very poor impression.

To use the terminology we created in Chapter Two; Martin, as the Proposer, does nothing to edify the Sponsor (his employer). His anxiety reflects badly on the company, and his lack of preparation could even be interpreted as a reflection on the general incompetence of the company.

Most significantly, he does nothing to make the presentation his own, to take control of the situation from the start – to *claim the stage*.

Now take a look at Naomi's start to her presentation.

The local Council has been keen to support local business initiatives and has offered a meeting room at its offices as a venue for the event. Tea and coffee are served at the back of the room and the chairs are set out in rows.

Naomi has arrived early and found someone who would move the chairs that were at the back of the room, down to the front, almost up to the table from which she will speak. This has reduced the distance between her and the front row, which she knows the audience will probably leave empty.

She places her notes on the table at the front, together with water and a drinking glass. Once she's comfortable with the layout, she then circulates around the room, greeting the guests and also meeting up with the president of the Women in Business group who will read the short introduction that Naomi has prepared in advance.

When the meeting starts and the president has introduced her, Naomi walks to the front of the room and takes her place behind the table. She pauses and looks around smiling.

She makes eye contact first with her colleague, Denise, who is sitting halfway down the room on the left, and then looks across to her assistant Jo, who is on the other side of the room, towards the front. Then she takes a breath ...

'Good afternoon.'

She pauses again, briefly.

'I am delighted to have this opportunity to share what I have been learning about the Government's new taxation proposals in respect of capital investment.'

And she goes on with a well-prepared and clearly delivered presentation. Right from Naomi's first words, the audience already has a sense of her gravitas. She has established her authority in the eyes of the audience. They can see her standing at the front and connecting with them, catching the eye of her two strategically-placed colleagues to give her more confidence.

By arranging to have them seated to both left and right, she has ensured she will speak to both sides of the room so that everyone in the audience feels included.

Before she started speaking, she paused and smiled. It's a momentary thing, but it *claims the stage*. It is such a simple act, but it immediately brands her as a professional.

Don't overdo it, or you can look self-conscious or even arrogant. Just let your demeanour and attitude show that you:

Are genuinely pleased to be there.

Want to connect and converse with the audience.

Will share something that is relevant to them (the WIIFY factor).

And ... remember that you are there to *change their mindset*.

While Naomi has been in control from the moment she arrived, Martin's failure to create his own comfort zone has got him off on the wrong foot.

... means never having to say you're sorry

A golden rule of speaking out is that you should (almost) never apologize.

Be proud of who you are and what you represent. If the Proposer and the Sponsor come across well, you will have prepared the ground for the Issue and the Message. Martin fails to create his comfort zone, and then his flood of apologies drags down the company and diminishes the perceived value of his message.

You must always be proud of what you have to say and of the visuals, props and other materials that you have put together to illustrate your presentation.

Martin has apologized about everything and made it clear that he wasn't properly prepared with his presentation material. The point here is that the guests couldn't have known what he planned to say, so they wouldn't have known if he said something different or whether the visuals that he had were as clear as he intended.

By admitting his lack of adequate preparation, he reveals a lack of respect for the importance of the meeting – and in doing so, he has insulted his guests.

At the offices of some companies, a business meeting starts with a large cafetière of freshly brewed coffee and a plate of handmade biscuits, and with bottles of both still and sparkling mineral water on the table. At other offices, beverages of indeterminate flavour come from a vending machine.

There's no need to apologize if your corporate culture falls into the latter category; you're in good company with some of the largest multi-nationals around the globe. While it is only a modest investment for any company to offer generous hospitality to guests, there are some visitors who might view such details as extravagance and unnecessary expense.

I struggled in my years in a London advertising agency between some clients on the one the hand, who expected a lavish lunch every time they came to London for a meeting, and clients on the other hand, who looked around our smart offices and the fresh flowers in reception and commented that it was the clients who were paying for such trimmings and that *they* never had flowers in their own factory offices.

But there are welcome touches of hospitality that don't cost money.

While it may be difficult to reserve car-parking spaces for visitors, it certainly creates a favourable impression if visitors don't have to spend ten minutes looking for a space and then walk through the rain to reach reception.

I shall never cease to be shocked by my local private hospital, where the only spaces that are convenient to the main entrance have large signs stating that these are reserved for consultants. Patients are directed to an overflow car park 50 yards away. It makes you wonder who is paying, and also whether a person who is unwell might find the walk uncomfortable.

The list of what Martin could and should do differently is a long one, and even if it took up the rest of this chapter, you would probably still have your own comments to add.

There is an old English saying, '*the devil is in the detail*', meaning that if the small things are overlooked they can cause serious problems. Martin did not have a list; he overlooked the '*alities*' and, worst of all, he kept apologizing.

When I am offered a disposable plastic cup of some disgusting hot beverage that masquerades as coffee at the exotic offices of a major software company in the Thames Valley, they never apologize – because instant freeze-dried is what they do.

Never apologize for what you are.

Anyway, I have a thing about coffee, as you may have guessed.

Hello, goodbye and amen

You saw how Naomi *claimed the stage*. The same principle applies when you finish speaking. You must draw the focus back to yourself and slow down.

On a much grander scale, think of a ceremony, or an event. Occasions don't suddenly end, they wind down and then come to a full stop. Reverting to one of our key messages, think of a conversation – it doesn't end in mid-flow.

So, when you come to the end of saying your piece, when you've reached the end of your Goldilocks and concluded with a resounding Beethoven, finish like Naomi:

'In the past twenty minutes or so, I've talked about the way taxation used to work, the way that the new legislation will affect all of us, and what we now need to do to minimize our exposure. In talking about this I touched on the worrying prospect of companies like yours and ours, facing punitive taxation when we seek to innovate by introducing expensive, but essential technology.

'We have to do everything we can to prevent that aspect of this proposal becoming Law. One way you can help is by adding your name to the petition at the back of the room. Of course, we realize that the Government has to find equitable ways of raising revenue. And we realize that the old system was both unfair and a disincentive to modernize our plant – but there can be no sense in a tax on innovation.

'I'm sure the Chamber of Commerce can count on the support of all of us here today, with its petition to the Government to reconsider this new tax. With the right fiscal framework, we can all flourish. And while nobody likes paying taxes, we could all look forward to increasing the overall amount of tax we pay when we are making increased profits that are generated from investment in innovation.

'So, please, sign up before you leave today.'

Naomi exudes authority without being patronizing or arrogant. Then she comes to the *amen* – the closing remarks which express her gratitude to the audience and give them the opportunity to show their acknowledgement of her.

> *'In closing, I would like to thank you all for the warm welcome and kind words of encouragement you have given me since I have taken up my role as FD of Amethyst. It's the first time a mother has held that role, and I hope that more of you who are mothers will find opportunities similar to mine for personal satisfaction in your own careers.*
>
> *'Madame President, it has been a pleasure to have the opportunity to talk today and I hope I've left enough time for questions.'*

Confidence is something you both earn and claim

Having given her audience what they wanted, an explanation of new tax proposals, Naomi uses the platform for a message of her own – an encouragement to women in management. She then steps out of the limelight and cedes control back to the chairman.

What's important and powerful is that by claiming the stage and owning the opportunity, Naomi established her personal authority. She held this, right through the presentation, and then added a personal, passionate and supportive note on which to close.

You've considered how Martin got it wrong. Now consider how Robert, Martin's colleague, would have handled it.

Explaining without apologizing

While Robert greeted his guests, his assistant Alex made sure everyone had tea and coffee and that they knew where the cloakrooms were situated. Once everyone was comfortable and had everything they needed, Robert took his position at the end of the table with a welcoming smile on his face.

> *'Good morning, I'm glad you could make it today to have a look at what we'll be unveiling at next month's trade fair. Obviously*

you're getting a sneak preview of a work in progress, but even at
this unfinished stage I'm sure you'll get a good enough idea of
what's coming up. We wanted to give you a unique opportunity
to express your interest before we open up to the general market.'

What you can see here is that whereas Martin was apologetic about
the unfinished state of his presentation, Robert has turned this to his
advantage. He hasn't thanked his audience for coming in the way
one might normally expect; instead, he has actually suggested that
they are privileged to be there and that he is giving them a *'unique*
opportunity'. This will not always be appropriate, but on this occasion
it is a shrewd tactic, designed to create a particular mood to
the occasion.

People are often uncomfortable about not thanking their audience,
but there are many situations when it is merely a formality and actually works to the detriment of the presentation. Ask yourself the
question: *'Who's doing whom a favour?'*

Sometimes there is a fifty-fifty balance to mutual advantage, as in
this social exchange:

'Thank you for coming over this evening.'

'Well, thanks for inviting us.'

That could equally well have been:

'Thank you for inviting us this evening.'

'Well, thank you for coming over.'

There are niceties of etiquette which demand a ritual 'thank you' like
the way that the English formally say *'How do you do,'* and expect
you to reply with the identical response of *'How do you do'*, rather
than any comment on your personal well-being. But empty, vacuous
phrases are just that, and if you incorporate them into a presentation
then you run the risk of diluting the power and effectiveness of what
you want to say.

Naomi doesn't thank the President in either her opening or closing
remarks; she expresses her pleasure to be there, which *implies*

gratitude – but if we are objective about it, we can rightly assume that the Women in Business network were grateful to have Naomi as a speaker. Naomi does, however, make a point of thanking the attendees for the way that they have welcomed her into the business community.

Expressions of thanks from the platform is another of those areas – like edification – where there is a balance to be struck. And if you think about it consciously, rather than just with the conventional automatic responses, you will improve the quality of your delivery.

Back to Robert's handling of this presentation. I am sure that by now you can guess how he will continue:

> 'What we have to show you today is:
>
> > An overview of the way the total market is developing.
> >
> > A look at where you and we have both been missing out.
> >
> > The way that we propose to attack this and give you the opportunity to fight back.
> >
> > Then, there's a bit of an extra incentive if we can work something out together before next month's big event.'

There's the classic Goldilocks plus Beethoven: the context, the issue and the solution – with the added clout of something extra to clinch the deal.

Both of these examples are for presentations to small meetings. Where you are on the platform at a larger event, there are other considerations which we shall look at in the next chapter.

Summary

Sorry and thank you

While there will be exceptions to this rule, it is appropriate to apologize only for genuine failings or shortcomings – and even then, only if they are clearly obvious.

Be proud of who you are and what you have to say. An apology diminishes you and your message. Furthermore, it suggests to your audience that you are ill-prepared.

It is similarly demeaning to express an excess of gratitude. Always be polite, but constant 'thank-yous' are as inappropriate as constant apologies. How many times have you cringed at Oscar ceremonies when the recipient has become embarrassing in his or her protestations of eternal gratitude to everyone?

It is possible to combine humility and gratitude, and at the same time to acknowledge pride in personal achievement.

When you are making a presentation and feel you ought to be thanking someone, think hard about *why* you want to say it. Don't give in if it's just an automated response.

Claim the stage

A professional takes time to create the right mood by taking a moment to pause and claim the stage before starting to speak.

Amen!

This is the other book-end to claiming the stage.

Slow down as you draw your presentation to a close, so that your proposals and recommendations are clear and memorable. This way you create impact with your ending, just as you did with your opening.

13

Basics of stagecraft

Fortress Lectern or free-form choreography

As the day approached for the last round of electioneering, Grunt still had worries about his ability to look confident. The mural that would be the visual aid to his speech was completed, and the level ground in front created a natural stage – but Grunt was worried about feeling exposed. He tried to explain his fears to Tork:

> *'It looks good, Tork, but I'm concerned about being a bit shaky. I'd rather like to feel a sense of safety, something to hold on to just in case I get a bit wobbly. So I think that pillar on the left is where I should stand when I'm talking.'*

Tork sighed and wondered how to explain to Grunt that he would diminish his presence if he was half-hidden:

> *'Grunt, you want people to see you.'*

> *'But they can see me!'*

> *'No they can't! You can see them all right; you've got a clear view of the entire hillside. But all they can see of you is your head and shoulders projecting above the top edge of that rock. It looks as if you're in hiding, taking cover, and waiting for a mammoth you can spear.'*

Grunt takes cover

'Well, no, err, I'm not hiding – but it does feel more comfortable here than it does if I stand out in the middle of the area. I feel so exposed if I do that.'

'Good!'

'What do you mean, good?'

'Well, the whole idea of these election rallies is that people get to know you, that they see who you really are, and they can't do that if you take cover and hide! People want to SEE the person they're voting for. They want to feel confident that they can trust you, put their faith in you, know that you are a brave person who will look after them if there are difficulties.

'They don't want someone who's hiding behind a rock. All you have to do is stand to one side. You can still rest your arm on it if you want to. Just let them see you and don't block the communication.'

Grunt finds a comfortable compromise

Some speakers cling to the sides of the lectern for dear life. In the conference industry, this practice has given birth to the phrase 'Fortress Lectern'.

Speakers do this because they have their notes, their script, or their laptop on the lectern – or because that's the way the stage has been lit to throw a spotlight on to the area around the lectern.

But the lectern isn't a pulpit to preach from. Nor is it a throne of authority from which to lay down the law, even if some countries do embellish the lectern with a large presidential seal on the front.

A lectern is merely a stand where you can put stuff you might need to refer to. It's no more and no less than that.

When you move away from the lectern, you increase your connection with the audience, provided that you can stay – literally – in the limelight. That's something you need to check out beforehand with the technicians at the venue, to ensure that you don't finish up either standing in the shadows or blocking the projection of any Audience Support materials onto the screen.

And just because the word 'lectern' comes from the Latin word for reading, it doesn't mean that you have to stay rigidly behind the lectern to follow your script line by line.

How to read your speech without just standing there

The French writer Victor Hugo is generally credited with saying that writing was '*like speaking without being interrupted*'.

By the same token, reading a speech is a way of forcing the audience to hear what they might otherwise read, while at the same time denying them the ability to skip and skim.

Some speeches stand the test of time, but only a very small proportion of the volumes of presentations that are delivered each year survive further than the handouts. Consequently, it doesn't generally make a lot of difference if there are minor differences between the exact words you speak and the printed words in the handouts.

When you first started to read at school, you worked it out word by word, your nose one inch from the page, stumbling, perhaps, when the word was multi-syllabled and breathing a sigh of relief when you reached the bottom of the page. Soon your eye could capture whole phrases, and after a while whole sentences, so that by the time you moved up to Big School it was not difficult to read silently and quickly. You could even read out loud in a clear and fluent voice, if you were called to do so.

To deliver your presentation as a scripted speech, all you need to do to achieve a professional standard, without being locked up in Fortress Lectern, is to take your reading skills one step further than has hitherto been necessary.

Even if you don't recognize that it is a significant skill, you have already learnt to speak one sentence while you eyes are absorbing the next. All you need to do now is to go slightly further, and let go of the security blanket of always having your eyes on the page.

178

It takes only split seconds for your eyes to capture the phrases; for the rest of the time you can look up, and look around at your audience. With practice – you always knew there would be a business benefit in reading bedtime stories to your children – you will find that your eyes can be mostly directed to the audience.

Once you've got the hang of this, you can confidently stand to the side of the lectern and simply glance across at your script whenever you need a prompt.

This is how many speakers work. They have a defined script that needs to be issued as a hand-out or published after the event, but they are sufficiently familiar with what they want to say that they can use their script as a prompt, rather than as a working text.

The leap of faith

I struggled for a long time with the next step. I would spend hours in my writer mode, crafting literary phrases, and then I would be terrified that I would forget it all when I came to speak.

What I always forgot was that the audience didn't have a copy of my script, and that there was no point in standing there, trying to remember my lines. What I had to do, rather, was to deliver my thoughts in a clear and convincing way, without worrying about the exact turn of phrase that I might have crafted on the keyboard.

The next step in developing your stagecraft is to realize that since your eyes are capturing just the key words in a paragraph, you don't need a complete word-for-word script. What you do need are simply those key words.

Yes, there's a skill in choosing which words to write down. But like all these skills, it just takes a little practice to turn a script into cue cards, and be able to deliver a presentation that matches up pretty well with the full version that you intend to issue as a handout.

Once you've weighed anchor and moved away from the safe haven of the lectern, there's a whole stage to sail across. You can use the area for useful visual clues as you tell your story, just as Tork teaches

Grunt to divide his presentation between the men and the women in the audience.

Left, right and centre

Tork decided that it was time to get Grunt to use the whole platform to ensure he connected with the whole audience. Grunt was standing in the centre of the area and began to enjoy the sense of performance:

'I see what you mean, Tork, this feels really good – and you're right, I was a bit hidden before, over there. I don't feel I'm hiding away now.'

'And who are you talking to? Who do you feel you'd be addressing, standing there?'

'Well, everyone! But especially the ones in the middle, I suppose.'

Tork jumped up and joined Grunt on the level area so he could give him clear instructions.

'The thing is, Grunt, if you stand there then, as you say, you have an excellent connection with the people in the middle. But the people at the edges are going to feel left out. So you need to move around a bit.'

Grunt immediately started pacing to and fro, reciting the opening lines that he had prepared.

He hadn't got far before Tork stopped him.

'That's no good! You don't make a connection with anyone if you just march across the stage. Don't talk and speak at the same time.'

'Don't talk and speak at the same time? That sounds a bit strange; it's what you and I do all the time when we're setting off across the lowland. We always say it's the best time for having a decent discussion, just walking along peacefully.'

'Yes, Grunt. But that's when there's just the two of us, and we're talking to each other. When you're here making your presentation, you have to be talking to the people in the audience.'

Tork demonstrated what he meant by striding across the stage talking to himself.

> 'You see, Grunt, there's no way I can go up and down like this and connect with the audience. But what I can do is to stand over here and address them, then walk across to another area when I want to make a different point. Then people connect the fact that I have moved across here with the fact that my speech has moved on, too.'

Grunt's face lit up as he understood the point that was being made.

> 'So, I could talk about things affecting the men, while I am over on one side – and then move over to the other side to talk about things that affect the women.'

> 'Exactly, and it helps people to compartmentalize their thinking as they see different points in your presentation being made from different physical positions on the platform.'

This technique – much beloved of NLP practitioners – works very well in exactly the way that Tork and Grunt have described. It's not a difficult point to remember, either, because the language that you may well be using gives you an immediate clue. When you say ...

> 'Right, let's move on to the next point,'

... you have a natural cue to do just that, and physically move on from one point on the stage to another, just as you move from one point in your argument to the next.

Using more than one location also works for talking about chronological spacing. The audience gets a clear sense of progression if you talk about past, present and future using an imaginary time-line that reaches from the past on your right (their left) to the future on your left (their right).

The reason for these specific directions is that from the perspective of the audience, the progression of time would be the same as they would read a line of text – from left to right.

This piece of stagecraft is particularly powerful, and is such an easy one to use because it feels very natural to move your own physical position while you talk about moving forwards or backwards in time.

Arms and the man

'What do I do with my hands?'

Grunt asked Tork, looking at him inquisitively.

'I get this idea of not hiding behind that rock, and I follow the logic of moving around to make different points in my presentation, but what about my hands? Where do I put them?'

Tork smiled:

'Grunt, just forget about them. Don't think about them. You don't normally think about what to do with your hands; it's only when you're in front of your audience that you become conscious of them. So, forget about them. Just leave them hanging at the end of your arms, where they usually are.'

Grunt thought for a moment while the words sank in.

'What d'you mean, where they usually are? Do you have detachable hands or something? Of course my hands are at the end of my arms! I just don't know how to feel comfortable.'

'I'm telling you, honestly, Grunt. If you think about your hands they'll be a problem. If you forget about them and concentrate on having that conversation with the audience, you'll find that your hands take care of themselves. Trust me, that's how it works.'

Most people become self-conscious when they stand up to speak, walk out in front of an audience, or are put on the spot in a public situation. Some people lock their hands together uncomfortably; others will wave them about in an attempt to overcome their nerves through gestures.

The basic rule is to start by leaving your arms by your side with your hands just hanging there. After some practice, you'll realize that you're not thinking about your hands and arms and that they really can take care of themselves.

The next step is to learn to use gestures in the course of your presentation.

Mediterranean people don't have a problem using their hands, arms, shoulders and whole upper body to communicate their message in a presentation or speech. However, one of the detrimental effects of globalization is that some of the natural liveliness and animation of their traditional style of communication has been dulled and dampened when executives from Southern Europe have tried to conform to what they perceive as the corporate norm.

If you have a Mediterranean heritage yourself, please don't start thinking that you have to be dull and boring to be respected in the corporate world! Body language can add to your presentation just as much as a clever turn of phrase. Gestures can add emphasis and elicit empathy and understanding from the audience.

What doesn't work is when the gestures are forced – or worse still, over-simplistic. You can safely afford to use expansive gestures when you are speaking, provided that you remember to match the scale of your gestures to the size of the audience. When you are talking to a small group, limit the extent to which you gesticulate. On the other hand, where you are addressing a large audience, small gestures will add nothing, and you can afford to be dramatic without being perceived as being as over-the-top.

Prompts and sign-language

Many managers and presenters have chosen to add a basic course in Neuro-Linguistic Programming to their portfolio of business attributes. While many of these skills are powerful in the hands of an expert, they can be dangerously off-putting when they are utilized by someone less competent. The general idea is that NLP gestures will make a clear connection between the spoken word and the associated part of the body. Hence ...

'If you look at this closely, you will see that ...'

183

... might be accompanied by the speaker raising her right index finger to her right eye.

And a really clumsy example ...

> *'Have any of you felt the same way?'*

... could be accompanied by the speaker's hand indicating the area around the heart ('feeling') and a gesture to the audience followed by a raised hand – which asks the audience to participate by raising a hand.

Once or twice I have seen this technique used effectively – but time and again I find that I wince, and at that point I switch off!

I welcome interactivity between the platform and the audience. But I resent clumsy and gauche invitations for participation.

'Morning all!'

Whenever I am in an audience, being asked by a presenter to consider a serious proposition, which is being put forward with the intention of changing my mindset, I really don't believe that I become any more receptive by being persistently invited to interact in audience participation.

Not that audience participation is necessarily inappropriate, but generally speaking you don't want to be like a late night game show; you want to be more like a serious discussion programme. That's the difference.

This takes us right back to the WIIFY factor in Chapter Three: you must know your audience, and be sure they understand *why* you think what you are saying could be of interest to them.

Some presenters like to begin their session with an over-enthusiastic *'Good Morning!'*

When I'm in the audience and, together with a few others around me, I grunt a grudging acknowledgement to this greeting, we would really like to think that the presenter could take the hint and move on. But no!

The presenter often then takes this as a cue for an even louder and even jollier '*GOOD MORNING!*' To which we are morally obliged to reply with a faint attempt at similar volume and grimace or risk being branded as a difficult and dozy group. I don't like to be reminded too severely of my shortcomings, especially when the reaction is coming from someone who is asking for my attention and wants to change the way I think about things.

Surrender, and asking for trouble

By the time I left Big School at the age of 18, I had grown out of putting my hand up in class. This is not to say that I won't step forward and volunteer when anyone asks for my participation, but the unbridled enthusiasm of fingers reaching ceiling-wards isn't a gesture I readily associate with.

You want your audience to be relaxed and receptive, so don't make them feel uncomfortable! You only have to look at the way some audiences respond to the speaker by timidly raising a wrist to shoulder level to see just how uncomfortable the speaker is making them feel.

Barristers in the Crown Court will not ask any question to which they do not already know the answer. Unless you are at a revivalist meeting or a pop concert, don't ask a question and expect an answer. Use questions, but use them cannily.

Rhetorical questions are a key element in a presentation because they get the audience thinking, they challenge the audience to know the answer, they persuade the audience to consider issues that they may not previously have taken seriously.

Ask a question by all means – but save your audience the pain of participation by giving them the answer yourself. Answering your own questions is the best way to ensure that you get the answer you want!

Creating real interactivity

With expert coaching from Raj, Jacqui got off to a strong start when she launched into her presentation in Las Vegas. There had been an excellent response to Amethyst's invitation to 'Tea at the Ritz' and there was an air of curious anticipation as Jacqui took the microphone:

> *'I'm delighted that so many of you have decided to sample* Tea at the Ritz *today – and I hope that my colleagues and I manage to meet with all of you at some time in the next hour or so. I'm just going to take 15 minutes of your time now, and then please stay around and chat for as long as you like. The room is ours until seven.*

> *'I realize that you're curious to know what this is all about, so let me ask you a few questions about what's happening to our industry. Up to a few years ago, people looked to department stores and specialist retailers when they wanted travel goods. But today, where are many of them finding that holiday suitcase or overnight bag?*

> *'The Internet?*

> *'Supermarkets?*

> *'Special offers in glossy magazines?*

> *'The answer is – in all of these. And is it hurting your trade? Yes of course it is!*

> *'And what is it doing to our business? We've traditionally been seen as a supplier of top quality luggage. Our prestige hangs not only on our products but also on the reputation of the outlets through which we reach our market.*

> *'How do we handle this change in distribution? Are we doomed to decline, or are we looking at a new opportunity?'*

Jacqui has asked six key questions:

1. Where are customers finding that holiday suitcase or overnight bag?
2. Is this hurting your trade?
3. What is it doing to our own business?
4. How do we handle this change in distribution?
5. Are we doomed to decline?
6. Are we looking at a new opportunity?

Jacqui provides answers to only two of these questions; for the rest, she leaves the answer hanging in the air and teases the audience with their realization that she will reveal the answers in the next few minutes.

But Jacqui has other plans. She has already spoken to some of her key customers and now approaches one of them:

'Georgina, you're the senior buyer for Hubbards, which is one of the most important department store groups in the UK. I know for a fact that your experiences will mirror those of many of your colleagues here in the States and elsewhere. Would you say that your share of the travel goods market is declining?'

Georgina rose to the occasion and replied confidently:

'I'm not telling my competitors and colleagues anything they don't know already if I say that you're absolutely right in your opening remarks. Hubbards maintains its reputation for the quality and competitiveness of its whole range. But there are new channels to market that didn't exist before and these are taking a significant share of the market.

'It's not affecting the prestige products – but it's definitely hitting the budget end of the market. I'm sure anyone here would say the same.'

All around the room there were nods of agreement. Jacqui continued:

'Thank you, Georgina. I know from the reactions around the room that I've touched on something that's an issue for everyone here today. And now it's time to explain why we chose a tea-party as the theme of today's get-together.

'It's because we all want our slice of the cake ...'

... and with that, Jacqui launched into the main part of her presentation.

Questions are a great way to get the audience thinking. They are especially effective if, like Jacqui, you can home in on the questions that they are already asking themselves and each other.

Jacqui knew Georgina well enough to know that she would rise to the occasion. The effect of her involvement and the confirmation that she gave to Jacqui's basic premise created the perfect foundation on which Jacqui could build her proposition.

This is interacting with the audience at its best. You are using the audience to support your argument, by giving them the opportunity to say it all for you.

Jacqui can now build on this initial rapport as she talks about the challenges and opportunities that both they and their distributors are facing.

She has promised them that she will talk for no more than 15 minutes, and as the only speaker she is in control and can keep her eye on her timing. However, if you are one of a number of speakers, timing can be an issue.

Knowing when to stop

Speakers who end on time will immediately earn the approval of the audience. So, I would advise two simple rules on timing:

1. If you start on time, finish on time, or
2. If the programme is running late, negotiate with the facilitator or, failing that, with the audience, as to what time your piece will end.

A good, professional moderator or conference chairman will take overall responsibility for time-keeping – but they will rely on cooperation from speakers to make this happen.

If you find yourself going on stage ten minutes late for a 30 minute presentation, don't feel that it's your job to take decisions about what to do with your presentation; ask the person in charge. A simple request takes the responsibility off your shoulders and demonstrates your professional approach to the task in hand.

The conversation might go something like this:

> *'Madame Chairman, before I start, I can see that we are running a few minutes behind schedule; what time would you like my slot to finish?'*

You have now put the responsibility firmly on the shoulders of the chairman. She can take the decision as to whether the presentations need to be curtailed or whether there are other opportunities to shave minutes off other items on the agenda. In this situation, she might propose something along these lines:

> *'It would be very helpful if we could get back on track. If you could shave five minutes off your presentation, and if I then cut the coffee break by five minutes, that will mean that we can start the next session on time. Can you manage that?'*

This gives you the opportunity to rescue a potentially tricky situation:

> *'Certainly – and if I do have to limit the question time at the end, then I'll be happy to answer any points the audience may have during the coffee break.'*

It is more than simple good manners: it earns you the respect of the audience and projects you in a very professional light.

With this in mind, it is good practice to know where you could shave 20 per cent off your presentation, should the need arise.

Often this can be achieved very simply by cutting out the Q&A session – but if you are prepared for the possibility of other speakers overrunning, then you can tailor your timing so that you can still leave some reduced time for one or two questions.

Summary

Refining your 'platform skills'

Going into hiding

It is not for nothing that it is called 'Fortress Lectern' in the conference industry.

Many speakers hide behind the lectern; a habit that is encouraged by the fact that event organisers make it their standard practice to wire up a fixed microphone to the lectern.

The lectern is a barrier; you can still glance at your notes if you stand to one side.

Learning to read

With a little practice, you can read by glancing down at a script only occasionally.

With more practice, you can deliver a script from cue cards.

With time, you can say what you want to say simply using a few notes, in the knowledge that the audience do not have a copy of the script and won't know if you add or omit anything from your planned discourse.

Learning to move

Using different points in the room to make different points in your presentation will anchor the differences through visual connection. Choreography can also be used to emphasize chronology and change.

Learning to gesticulate

Don't fiddle with your hands. If in doubt, just 'hang loose'. When you want to use gestures to make a point, regulate the size of the gesture to the size of the audience. In a small group use small gestures – but when you have a big audience, be expansive.

Interacting with the audience

Don't embarrass your audience with long pauses, while you wait in anticipation of their response. Make sure you get the right answers by asking rhetorical questions and answering them yourself.

Keeping in time

Keep your contract with the audience to take only the time you have asked for. Where your presentation is delayed by others overrunning, respect your audience by asking the chairman for guidance, or by requesting the audience's permission before prolonging the tardiness of the agenda.

Conclusion

What happens next?

New beginnings

As the retiring chieftain, Alto was acting Returning Officer.

When the votes had been counted, he called the candidates to join him in front of the assembled tribe. A hush fell over the crowd as he started to announce the tally of votes – then a cheer erupted as he turned to congratulate Grunt on his landslide victory.

Grunt moved forward to acknowledge the plaudits and raised his hand to ask for quiet:

'*No more applause*! *No more speeches*! *And no more meetings*!

Grunt is elected

'When I started on this journey, Tork told me I would need a manifesto, and I thought it was some sort of badge I had to wear. Now I know that in one sense I was right: my name, my reputation and my personality hang on that manifesto.

'Every time you see me, you will see the manifesto: you will see the man who committed himself to making changes, and you will see the promises that I made, which were the basis for your decision to elect me.

'I showed you my vision, and you understood my perspective. You shared my view because that is the way that you wanted to see our future here on the mountain. Five years ago, we lived as separate tribes and life was hard. Then Wizpa and Chat brought their people to live with us. Life has been good and the future looks even better, thanks to the new skills that they brought with them.

'Thank you for sharing my vision. Thank you for all the encouragement you have given me through the past weeks. Thank you for pledging your support with your votes. Now we have plans to make, changes to introduce and work to do.

'Tonight we celebrate. Tomorrow the sun will come up on a new day, and together we will begin to create our new future.'

Grunt put into practice the basic rules of Goldilocks and Beethoven to construct a simple, off-the-cuff speech that was a clarion call to the assembled people. The validity of his words would be evidenced in his ability and determination to implement the plans of his manifesto.

The morning after

Every week executives, managers, trainers and officials make thousands of presentations in countries all around the world. And on the following Monday morning, their audiences return to their offices and do exactly what they were doing previously.

Many of the presentations will have failed because they simply communicated information and didn't have the clear intention of *changing the mindset* of the audience. Other presentations will have

193

failed because the audience simply *didn't see what was in it for them*. And a few presentations might have failed because the speaker's *delivery* wasn't all that it should have been.

When all is said and done, the delivery, the quality of your visuals and the way you keep scratching your ear are not the decisive factors in making an impact. It's your belief, it's the passion that you feel for what you say, and it's the way you've identified with the audience's perspective and values that will change their mindset.

In matters of the heart, nobody will ever love you unless you love yourself. When it comes to matters of business and organization, nobody will believe what you say unless you believe it yourself. And don't think that you can delude others; the likelihood is that you will reveal all the more clearly just how much you are deluding yourself.

The actions that follow the words

Presentations should be both a beginning and an end.

They mark the **end** of a preparatory phase of working out what needs to be done to make changes. At the same time, they mark the **beginning** of a phase of doing something positive to resolve a situation.

Presentations announce how you plan to make change happen the way you want it to, rather than let change happen and then react to whatever evolves and develops.

Time and again you will hear people deliver well-crafted presentations that are spoken with conviction and passion as they make a brave statement about the need for change. But then those same confident presenters are reduced to chattering incompetence by three simple words:

'Yes, but how ...?'

Don't ever risk making a presentation unless you have the plans in place for the next phase. Don't send out the troops without the logistical support in place. And never make promises that you cannot fulfil.

Postscript

Grunt fought his way through the crowd, shaking hands to left and right, till he finally reached Tork.

'Well, Grunt, you did it! Congratulations – and that was a great acceptance speech with just the right tone.'

'You're the one who taught me all those important lessons about connecting with the audience and being passionate about what I was saying and ... oh, everything. Well, thank you! Look, I want a quick word before the party begins.'

Tork and Grunt slipped away from the crowd and over the brow of the hill, just far enough to be out of earshot and have a private conversation.

'As I see it, Tork, the big question now is "What next?" I realize I've given people a vision, and I honestly believe that most people have bought into that, but we have to turn that vision into reality.'

'And you know, Grunt, there's something fundamental that we have to do if we're going to achieve that, and you know what I'm going to say, don't you?'

'Of course I do. It's one community made up of four tribes: yours, mine, Wizpa's and Chat's. We've all got our own way of doing things, our own traditions, our own cultures and somehow we need to merge and become one tribe.'

'Yes, Grunt, and in a generation or two that will be the reality, but you and I will be long since gone.

'Which is why I think we should talk to Chukka, the young hunter. You and I are both closely identified with the way things were; we're the older generation. We can look after the fears of our generation; what we need is someone who will embrace the hopes of the next generation.'

Grunt smiled, Tork was right. Success would depend on the next generation.

> '*I am the new chieftain, you'll be my right hand man and I think you're absolutely right to propose Chukka as part of the team.*'

Tork shook Grunt's hand energetically.

> '*Fantastic! I'm so pleased you get the idea.*'

> '*It's not just an idea, it's a vision. You said we needed a vision and that's what I focused on in all my speeches. We've got a hundred days to show we're in business. Let's have a word with Chukka.*'

Chukka joins the leadership

They found Chukka smartening himself up for the party and they outlined what they had in mind for him. Chukka was shocked and took a moment to take it all in.

'When you were making your speeches, you made me change the way I look at things, that's why I voted for you. I could see you had ideas about our future as one strong and powerful super-tribe.'

Tork added:

'You know, I think it all came together because we could all see the benefit for ourselves, and we all started to look at things differently. Well done, Grunt!'

Grunt was pleased with himself, as he realized that he'd managed to changed people's mindset.

'Remember this, Chukka. Respect what other people want and need and they'll give you what you want and need.

'As long as you can see the other side's point of view, you'll be able to work it out. Show them the way, and help them choose. It's all about arrows, not bullets.'

Tork's eyes rolled heavenwards

'Goodness, Grunt, you sound like a politician. Chill out! Let's see if that brew is ready, I could use a drink.'

And off the three of them went into the sunset glow over the lake, in a mood of blissful ignorance, to face the realities of what would later be called Change Management.

Acknowledgements

As I started to work on this book, I drew heavily on my experience as a member of Bromley Speakers Club in Kent, which is affiliated to Toastmasters International (www.toastmasters.org). Here I learned speaking in a warm and friendly atmosphere and I went on to compete as a speaker internationally. It was that experience and learning, which gave me the grounding to write this book.

As a scriptwriter and subsequently a speaker-coach I have been frustrated time and again by corporate policies on the use of bullet-pointed slides. When I researched this book I became aware of a wind of change, with academics like John Sweller in Australia, Edward Rolf Tufte at Yale and Garr Reynolds in Japan. All three were espousing new thinking, and this was reflected by the output of Californians like Mark and Nancy Duarte in Mountain View and Cliff Atkinson in Los Angeles.

It was Cliff's book, *Beyond PowerPoint* that led me to the concept of the Goldilocks Principle and the Beethoven Imperative, which I now teach to executives looking for a better way to structure their presentations. My thanks go to all these people for the inspiration that I gained from their writing and their ideas.

The Book Cooks, Lesley Morrissey, Jo Parfitt and editor Fiona Cowan all followed their excellent work on *Tork & Grunt's Guide to Effective Negotiations* by reacquainting themselves with Tork, Grunt and the tribes. Julie Hargreaves gave invaluable advice and encouragement from the viewpoint of a novice speaker.

Martin Liu and Pom Somkabcharti at Cyan tolerated my persistent nagging emails and phone calls and I thank them for their support and encouragement. David Mostyn once again worked his cartoon magic with all the cave-people, and Anna Marie Buss created the PowerPoint images; many thanks to both.

I have only one more piece of advice for my readers. Remember the fifth risk of speaking out: If you don't do it, you'll never realize your potential.

About the author

Bob Harvey is the author of two highly entertaining and informative books on cutting-edge communication techniques:

> *Tork & Grunt's Guide to Effective Negotiations*
>
> *Tork & Grunt's Guide to Great Presentations.*

Bob graduated with an honours degree in Economics and is a Fellow of the Royal Society of Arts. In the past, he has held the title of UK Public Speaking Champion together with the title for Impromptu Speaking. His career has encompassed brand management, sales, writing for magazine columns and broadcasting.

Today, Bob specializes in designing, scripting and delivering all types of corporate communications. He set up his company, Messages into Words, to help businesses get their message across and has worked with many of the world's largest corporations in developing their corporate communications. He also runs extremely popular and successful workshops on communication techniques and personal management skills.

Bob can be contacted via his company's websites:
www.messagesintowords.com and **www.bobharvey.co.uk**

For those readers wishing to explore Tork and Grunt's world, please visit **www.TorkandGrunt.com**

Tork & Grunt's Guide to Effective Negotiations is a story told through the lives of Tork and Grunt and their fellow cave-people, because people have negotiated since cavemen fought for food. You negotiate at home and at work, at school and in retirement, but time and again this leads to conflict and disagreement because you can't see a way to find a mutually beneficial outcome.

In this book you'll discover how Tork and Grunt develop their Mammoth Strategies, which not only work for them and their tribe, but also work for modern-day scenarios like buying houses, planning holidays and getting promoted. The Mammoth Strategies include:

➤ Three rules and four criteria for successful negotiation
➤ The difference between positional and directional negotiation
➤ The six steps in the negotiation process
➤ The when, why, what, where and how of preparation
➤ How to establish your WAO – your walk-away option
➤ Working with issues, not personalities
➤ Effective tactics and rules for when the other side plays rough
➤ How to negotiate as a team

It's all about communication. Negotiation isn't about compromise. It's about listening to the other person and working out what they really want to achieve as well as being clear in your own mind about what you want. You will get what you want by finding a way to give the other person what they want.

ISBN 978-0-462-09923-1 / £9.99 Paperback